You Can Say F*ck In Here

Stories From The Couch

Dr. Katie Fields

SOUL PURPOSE
PUBLISHING

Edited by Jan Edwards www.janedwards.org

Published by Soul Purpose Publishing

https://soulpurposepublishing.com

Praise For You Can Say F*ck in Here

"A deep therapeutic dive, filled with challenges, delivered with ease and heightening self discoveries. These stories reveal how survival shapes identity—and how awareness begins to loosen its grip."
~ Edie S., EdS, LMFT, LMHC

"Raw, insightful, and deeply relatable, this book captures the subtle moments of therapy that quietly change everything."
~ Casey S.

"Part storytelling—part psychological mirror. I saw myself in many of the chapters, which made me think of my own life and challenges from a unique perspective."
~ Izabella T., PhD

"These stories challenge us to face the raw truth behind our choices and uncover the hidden triggers that shape our reactions."
~ Kassandra P.

"I would've never thought reading a book about counseling could be a page turner. I couldn't wait to read the next story. Self reflection plus humor—I highly recommend!"
~ Melanie C.

"An honest and vulnerable invitation into the therapy room. Katie reminds us that growth doesn't happen only for the client—it transforms the therapist, as well. Refreshing, human, and deeply genuine."

~ Kim P., MS, LMFT

Dedicated

to my husband,
who instantly saw the potential in this book's title
and used his voltage to encourage me to write it.

to my children,
whose precious invitations return me to my essence
and show me how to play again.

to my clients,
whose courage and willingness to be vulnerable
continue to inspire me.

to Dina, my publisher,
who gently held my hand
and patiently walked beside me through this process.

and to this book,
which met me on the couch in so many ways,
holding me while I found my truth.

We survived by becoming who we needed to be.

We heal when we risk being who we truly are.

Acknowledgements

Writing about therapy is a strange task.

The most meaningful work I have ever participated in happens in private spaces, during conversations that were never meant to leave the room. This book exists, because hundreds of people trusted me with pieces of their lives—moments of honesty, grief, humor, fear, and courage that unfolded across weeks, months, and sometimes years of therapeutic work.

While the stories in this book are fictional, drawn from composites of true moments, with identifying details altered to protect confidentiality, the emotional truths they contain belong to the many people who have allowed me to witness their humanity. If you have ever sat across from me in the therapy room, please know that your willingness to show up—imperfectly, honestly, and sometimes reluctantly—shaped the therapist and writer I have become. I am truly forever grateful for this.

I am deeply grateful to the colleagues, mentors, teachers, and theorists who helped form the clinical foundation of my work. The traditions of psychotherapy, trauma research, and developmental psychology have given language to experiences that so many people struggle to understand on their own.

Just as meaningful were the people who showed me what authenticity could look like in practice. One influential mentor—who was also my first IFS therapist—gave me permission to show up authentically and modeled it. Her office looked like something straight out of a Tim Burton film. The colors were red, black, and white, and a shrunken head with an open mouth filled with tiny slips of paper hung at the door for visitors to take. I remember thinking, I didn't know therapy offices could look like this. Thanks to her and the work I've done with my Self, I now enjoy my own witchy cottage vibe, complete with cats, bunnies, and a tiny maltipoo.

I especially want to thank Isabell, who jolted me in the summer of 2022. In trying to prepare for an interview about my work with couples and infidelity, I was unexpectedly activated. She was inviting me to loosen up, to play with the process. Instead, I froze. I cried. I felt exposed, like an imposter who'd been revealed, getting it wrong, and unable to recover by performing my way through it. I left feeling like I had blown the opportunity, and I carried that shame for months—maybe even years. That moment broke something open. I began to see how often I was performing my work, instead of inhabiting it—how my compulsion to do it well was quietly interfering with my ability to actually be in it. It was an oh f*ck moment that I will never forget.

I also want to appreciate my Reiki master, who provided a similar realization in 2024. After years of studying and practicing, I saw that I had been going through the motions—doing the steps, saying the words, trying to get it right—without fully trusting what was actually moving through me. I saw a vision of myself using a toy doctor's kit, instead of developing my real abilities. It was humbling. And painful. It disrupted trust. Yet it was also inviting something more honest of me. Reiki has been a meaningful part of my shift.

I want to thank my soul sister, friend, and colleague, who I spoke with through each of these moments, and many others. We share similar patterns and a kind of unspoken understanding of each other's protective strategies. She is the kind of person who understands you without requiring much explanation. Together, we have explored ourselves, our marriages, our parenting, our work, and the cosmos. I am deeply grateful for her love, her honesty, and for the safety we've built over time to be fully human with each other.

I am equally grateful to the friends and loved ones who tolerated the strange process of writing this book—reading and rereading drafts, patiently waiting through long stretches of me being absorbed in the work, revising, questioning, and occasionally staring off into the abyss, trying to find the right stories.

I'm also immensely grateful for this process and for my willingness to go through it. This has felt therapeutic in the best and worst ways. Writing a book of this sort is a process of discovery and introspection. It took me through so many layers of myself. Working with a skilled and professional editor was exposing, painful—seemingly relentless at times—and necessary for me to meet the loose ends of me, still asking to be seen and felt. Jan— thank you for your sensitivity and grace as I moved through this experience.

Lastly, sharing this book with others was so much more intimate than I could have ever imagined. Those who read it will know more about me than some of my closest loved ones. To you, the reader, thank you for your willingness to explore what's inside.

Foreword

There are books that inform. Books that entertain.

And in rarer cases, books that feel alive—quietly initiating healing, growth, and transformation through moments of recognition.

And here we are.

*You Can Say F*ck In Here* draws you into the lives of its characters in a way that lingers long after the final page. This is its quiet brilliance. Rather than confronting you directly, it slips past the resistance we all carry—the instinct to self-protect, to curate the stories we tell ourselves about who we are. Instead, it invites reflection through the safety of someone else's experience.

Each vignette becomes a mirror—but not an obvious one. There is no instruction manual here, no heavy-handed analysis. Instead, there are moments of illumination. Epiphanies. The subtle, disarming recognition of, Oh... that's me.

The therapist in these pages does not fix. She reveals. And in doing so, she captures something essential about being human: change rarely begins with grand insight, but with small, often quiet moments of realization that shift how we see ourselves.

There is something both intimate and disarming about being invited into the therapy room. Many of us will never sit across from a therapist and say the things that live just beneath the surface—the fears we justify, the patterns we repeat, the stories that quietly organize our lives. And yet here, we are given that access.

You begin as an observer. Curious. Slightly removed. And then, gradually, something shifts.

A familiar pattern emerges. A line lands differently than expected. You feel something tighten in your chest—subtle, but unmistakable.

And, without realizing it, you are no longer just watching.

You are in the room.

This book offers a rare kind of encounter—brief glimpses into lives that somehow leave a lasting imprint. You will see yourself here. Not all at once, and not in obvious ways, but in fragments. In patterns. In moments that echo something familiar within you.

What is most striking is the compassion woven throughout. Even in moments of frustration, resistance, or contradiction, there is an underlying understanding that we are all doing the best we can with what we know—until we know more.

And perhaps, that is what this book ultimately offers.

Not answers, but awareness.
Not solutions, but perspective.
Not judgment, but recognition.

And, with recognition comes something powerful—the possibility, and the courage, to change.

It is rare to encounter a practitioner who brings this level of self-awareness into their work. What distinguishes Katie is not only her clinical skill, but her willingness to continually turn inward—to examine her own patterns with the same honesty she invites from others.

As someone who has spent over 16 years working as an acupuncturist, hypnotherapist, and intuitive, I have seen what separates a competent healer from an exceptional one. The difference is not technique—it is integrity. The capacity to do one's own work, to remain in an ongoing process of growth and self-examination.

Katie embodies that commitment.

It is what makes her presence in the room both grounded and transformative—and what makes this book feel as alive as it does.

Her work reflects the standard we should all be seeking when we allow someone into the deepest, most vulnerable parts of our lives.

~ Marisa Fanelli
Licensed Acupuncturist
Certified Hypnotherapist
Founder of Find Your Healers

Preface

If you have ever been to therapy, you know the feeling of a waiting room.

You sit in a chair that doesn't quite belong to you yet. Maybe there's a plant in the corner next to the sound machine and, perhaps, a closed door that you know will soon open.

You may be rehearsing what you plan to say—or wondering if you should say it at all.

A few years ago, the title of this book appeared in my life before I was ready for it.

*You Can Say F*ck in Here*

At the time, I wasn't a writer, which made holding that title feel a little like sitting in that waiting room chair—close to something, but not quite belonging there yet.

The title came out during a conversation with my husband. I was telling him about something I had been noticing in the therapy room—how often clients softened their words or edited themselves halfway through a sentence.

My husband is not someone who censors himself. I'm learning to love that about him.

So, when I joked, "Maybe I should write a book called *You Can Say F*ck in Here,*" he didn't laugh.

He looked at me with his serious eyes and said, "You should do that. That would be a bestseller."

Since I wasn't a writer, I pushed the idea aside.

But the idea had already found its way into the therapy room.

I started telling clients that I was going to write a book called, *You Can Say F*ck in Here,* usually right after I noticed them using the safer word, while the actual word hovered just behind.

And every time I said it, something in the room would shift.

A breath would release.

A sentence would finally land.

What I slowly began to realize was that people often come to therapy carrying the same instinct they use everywhere else—the instinct to edit themselves in order to stay acceptable, safe, or connected.

Permission changes that.

Around the same time, while circling the process of writing this book and trying to declutter my life, I began working with my therapist, Shannon.

Before Shannon, I worried that if I didn't seem like I had all of my shit together, a therapist might silently think I wasn't good enough—or safe enough—to be a therapist.

So, I hid.

I knew how to make everything sound fine—even impressive. I was very good at explaining my life in ways that made it seem like I had it handled.

Eventually, I realized that I was avoiding myself. I was sabotaging my growth—and definitely not getting my money's worth in therapy.

I was doing myself a disservice.

So, in my very first session with Shannon, I outed myself.

I told her about my habit of hiding in therapy.

She asked if it was okay to call me out if she noticed it.

I said yes.

I was tired of my patterns keeping me from my potential.

I was ready.

Almost immediately, Shannon made me feel safe.

A few sessions in, she gently pointed out that I seemed burned out.

Something in me cracked open with relief.

I was burned out.

I had been scattering my energy, and things were starting to fall through the cracks. My worst nightmare was happening. I was failing—and being seen failing.

Instead of judging me, Shannon helped me slow down and understand what I was doing.

For the first time, I could see myself clearly.

The same patterns of protection that I helped clients notice every day were quietly shaping my own life.

Somewhere along the way, the idea of this book returned.

*You Can Say F*ck in Here.*

Writing it has stretched me in ways I didn't expect.

Somewhere in the process of telling these stories, I fell in love with being an author.

I also fell more in love with myself.

It turns out that writing a book can feel a lot like therapy.

Both ask you to sit with yourself long enough for something new to emerge—something longing to emerge.

So, if you're holding this book now, imagine that you're sitting in that waiting room chair.

Not because something is wrong with you, but because something in you is curious.

Who are you when you aren't protecting yourself, strategizing how to be okay in the world around you?

I've found that curiosity is often the beginning of honesty—

And the beginning of the journey.

My door opens for you.

Contents

Welcome

Welcome. Come in.

I'm glad you're here. Close the door and have a seat.

If you'd like, you can take your shoes off. Get comfortable.

I'll do the same.

Before we begin, I want to give you a sense of how I work—just enough for you to know what you're stepping into.

As I see it, most people don't come to therapy because something is wrong with them.

They come because something that once helped them survive no longer helps them live.

Most of us learned early what to do to stay connected, safe, and worthy of belonging.

Be impressive.
Be easy.
Be strong.

Be useful.
Be quiet.
Be needed.

Over time, these strategies become automatic, like a reflex.

And eventually, the ways we learned to stay connected can become the very ways we lose connection—with ourselves and others.

In therapy, we pay attention to those patterns.

Not to judge or eliminate them, but to understand what they've been trying to protect—and where and if they're still needed.

My licensure supervisor once told me that being a psychotherapist is like being a physical therapist—we're trying to help clients regain their range of motion.

When we get stuck in belief systems and patterns of behavior, we are limited in our perspectives and possibilities.

Sometimes it helps to think of these patterns as roles carried by different parts of us.

One part learned how to smooth things over.
One learned to stay ahead.
One learned when to disappear.
One learned how to take control.
Each developed for a reason.

Over time, certain parts become dominant. They step in quickly, automatically, and repeatedly—until we begin to mistake them for our identity rather than adaptations.

In this work, we're not trying to get rid of those parts.

We're getting to know them well enough to understand their role and their story, creating internal connection and appreciation. We're also allowing these parts to realize they are not alone and what was happening when they developed these roles, isn't happening now.

There are many ways to understand these inner systems and the strategies they develop. Some of the tools I draw from are:

Internal Family Systems therapy
Somatic parts work
Tarot
The Enneagram

You'll see pieces of each throughout the stories ahead.

Internal Family Systems helps us understand the multiplicity of the mind and the protective roles our parts take on.

Somatic work helps us listen to the body and notice how experience lives beneath language.

Tarot offers symbolic mirrors for the human journey.

And the Enneagram helps me organize these patterns into a cohesive map.

I don't use the Enneagram as a personality label.

I use it as a way of noticing where attention goes under pressure, the behaviors we reflexively rely on, and the strategies we use to navigate life.

You may notice tendencies to:

get things right
be liked
stay in control

avoid conflict
be needed
seek certainty
stand apart
stay strong
keep the peace

These aren't who you are.

They are patterns.

In my work, I'm less interested in your "type" than in understanding the protective systems shaping—and limiting—your life.

Underneath every pattern is something deeply human:

a need for connection,
a fear of losing it,
and a nervous system adapting accordingly.

The goal is not to define you.

It's to help you recognize yourself clearly enough that you gain more choice—and feel less driven by automatic strategies that once protected you.

Throughout this book, you may notice that vulnerability doesn't always look dramatic.

Often, it looks like:

a hesitation,
a breath held too long,
a sentence that almost gets spoken but doesn't.

Those are the moments we slow down around.

That's where the work lives.

And I want to be clear: I'm not outside of this.

Even writing these words, I can feel my own reflex to do this well—to sound clear, useful, competent. Those are my patterns.

I know many of the parts that organize my own behavior. I've studied them professionally, personally, and from the other side of the couch.

I remember one session in particular. My hands were folded tightly in my lap so I wouldn't gesture too much. My posture was straight. My voice measured. I was explaining something in a way that sounded articulate, organized... impressive.

My therapist waited quietly before saying:

"You're performing this."

My face went hot.

Immediately, my protective parts mobilized. I laughed. Clarified. Tried to sound even more thoughtful.

She didn't argue.

She just stayed.

And in that quietness, I noticed the effort it took to hold myself together—the pressure to remain composed, controlled, acceptable.

Underneath it was a fear I knew well:

not of falling apart, but of being seen before I was ready.

My parts believed that if I stopped performing competence, I might be criticized, rejected, or left alone.

There were no tears. No cinematic breakthrough.

Just the uncomfortable realization that I didn't know how to exist in the room without managing how I was perceived.

For me, vulnerability wasn't crying.

It was loosening my grip on being impressive—and not knowing what would happen next.

Therapy is private for a reason.

It is one of the few places left where you don't have to perform competence, certainty, ease, or strength in order to stay connected.

At least, that's the hope.

Some of the most therapeutic moments begin quietly.

The room goes still.

Your attention turns inward instead of outward.

Your shoulders drop slightly.

Your breath changes.

You start to say something, then stop yourself.

Your jaw tightens. Your hands curl. Something rises.

That's when I say:

"You can say f*ck in here."

And something finally releases.

Raw. Unedited. Honest.

That's emotional truth.

The stories ahead offer a glimpse into the kinds of moments that unfold in my work.

The clients in these pages may be wrestling with questions you know intimately yourself:

If I stop being who I learned to be, will I still be loved?
If I stop performing the role that kept me safe, will I still be ok?
Who am I without the pattern?

You'll also see my own humanity in the room—not as a therapist above the process, but as a person participating in it, with my own nervous system responding in real time.

Because therapy is not neutral territory.

It's a relationship.

People—and all their parts—negotiating safety together.

As we go, you may begin noticing your own reactions:

what pulls you in,
what you resist,
what tightens,
what softens,
what feels familiar.

You don't have to force insight from any of it.

Just notice.

That's often where change begins.

Not in dramatic breakthroughs,

but in small moments where something finally gets to be seen.

Writing this book feels a bit like that for me.

There's a part of me that wants it polished, airtight, beyond criticism.

And there's another part—the one who once sat rigid on that couch with her hands folded too tightly—that knows perfection can become another form of hiding.

So this is me, loosening my grip a little.

Allowing the real me to emerge.

Permission Slip
to say
fuck
in here

A Note On the Stories

These eighteen stories are composites drawn from my experience as a therapist and my personal journey in the world. Experiences have been blended across multiple individuals and therapeutic encounters. To protect those who have inspired them, identifying details have been altered. Histories are different. Strategies are different.

No story in this book represents a single client, session, or life circumstance exactly as it occurred. Yet, the conversations I'll share are faithful to the emotional truths that emerge in therapy—the questions people ask when they are trying to understand themselves, the patterns that slowly become visible over time, and the moments when something long held in place begins to shift.

Therapy is not a performance, and it is rarely as neat as a story. In real life, insight unfolds gradually. What you will see here are condensed moments—snapshots of the kinds of realizations that happen when people become curious about how they are showing up and whether that is still serving them.

I'm about to take you through a week in my office, eighteen sessions plus my own. This will really give you a feel for the kind of work I do.

The Ones

Audited at Intake

She sits down like we're in an interview.

"I'd like to ask you a few questions before we start," she says.

"Sure," I respond.

"Where did you go to school?"

I tell her.

"How long have you been practicing?"

I answer.

"Advanced training beyond your license?"

"Yes."

"In what?"

I summarize.

She nods, internally logging my answers.

"And what kind of therapy do you use?"

"I help you understand your patterns, the way you engage or disengage with your life. And then we practice listening to your body and attending to your nervous system."

"So, not just talking."

"Not just talking."

"What are your outcomes?"

"It depends on the client."

"Are you going to dig into my childhood?"

"Only when relevant."

A small exhale.

"And how do you know it's working?"

"You respond instead of react. Your body softens when it used to brace. You don't monitor yourself as much."

She doesn't comment. She's still monitoring.

"I've done therapy before."

"How was it?"

"It was fine."

Fine.

"I understood why I was doing things. I named my feelings."

"But nothing changed," I said.

"No. I still wake up tense. Replay conversations. Edit what I should've said."

Her jaw tightens.

"I don't want to waste another year."

My pattern catches it:
Waste.

"And what would change look like?" I ask.

"Relief."

"And how would you know you felt it?"

She pauses.

"I don't know. No one's asked me that."

We sit there for a moment.

"They either just listened," she continues, "or gave me skills that worked temporarily. Or they made interpretations."

"And that felt...?"

"Premature. Exposing."

"And then?"

"I shut down."

"I don't like someone thinking they know something about me before I've decided if it's accurate."

"You don't like someone having the upper hand."

"No."

"It also sounds like you hold therapists to a standard."

"I hold everyone to a standard."

"And yourself?"

She pauses.

"Yes."

I ask, "Do you have standards for therapy?"

Her eyebrow lifts.

"Don't waste time."

"Mm."

"Don't be dramatic. Don't overreact."

"Anything else?"

She pauses.

"Don't lose control."

"And swearing?"

"I'd rather not."

"You can say f*ck in here," I say.

She blinks.

"I don't need to."

"I know. But you can."

Silence.

"Now?" she asks.

"Why not?"

Annoyed.

"F*ck," she says.

Her words are clipped, contained.

We wait.

"Again?" I ask.

She rolls her eyes.

"Why?"

"Because you can."

She breathes.

"F*ck."

This one lands lower.

Her throat moves when she swallows.

"That feels unnecessary," she says, recovering.

"Maybe," I say. "Maybe unnecessary feels unsafe."

She straightens.

"I don't like chaos."

"I can see that. You prefer order."

"Yes. And logic."

"You believe if something is done correctly, it should work."

"Yes."

"And if it doesn't?"

"Something is wrong."

I nod.

"I'm going to offer something," I say. "You can reject it."

She nods once.

"There's a way of moving through the world that assumes that—if you regulate correctly, choose correctly, speak correctly—you should get the outcome you expect."

She remains still.

"And when you don't, you refine the method."

Her eyes narrow.

"That's rational."

"It is."

"And when vulnerability shows up before it's scheduled," I continue, "you critique it, tighten, correct."

Her jaw firms.

I hold the silence.

"I'm not making an assumption," I say, "I'm noticing a pattern."

"If therapy works when done right—and you are very good at doing things right—and you don't get relief..."

I let it hang.

Her fingers press into her thigh.

"...then the only variable left is you."

The air sharpens.

"That's reductive," she says immediately.

"Is it?"

"You're implying that I'm sabotaging myself."

"I'm suggesting that you might be controlling the conditions so tightly that nothing unpredictable or unaccounted for can contribute."

"That's not sabotage. That's responsible."

"Maybe."

She looks down.

A moment passes.

"I don't want to be the problem."

"I don't think you are," I say,

"I think you're participating."

"In what?"

"In preventing the one thing you say you want."

"Relief?"

"Yes."

"How?"

"By only allowing it on your terms."

She sits back. Still rigid.

"If that's me," she says, "what's the fix?"

I almost smile.

"There it is."

"What?"

"The reflex to fix."

She exhales sharply.

"That's not a flaw."

"No. It has worked."

"And now you're saying it's the issue."

"I'm saying that it might be keeping you stuck in some ways."

Her eyes gloss briefly.

"I don't like the idea that I'm participating in my own stuckness."

"I know."

She pauses.

"I don't want to do that."

Her voice thins.

"And I don't like that you're not intimidated by me."

That catches me.

I check in with myself.

"I'm not," I say.

She studies me.

"I thought you might try to impress me," she says.

"I considered it," I say with a smirk.

That earns a small smile.

At the end of the hour, she stands.

At the door, her hand rests on the knob.

"F*ck," she says softly.

This time it isn't compliance.

It's relief.

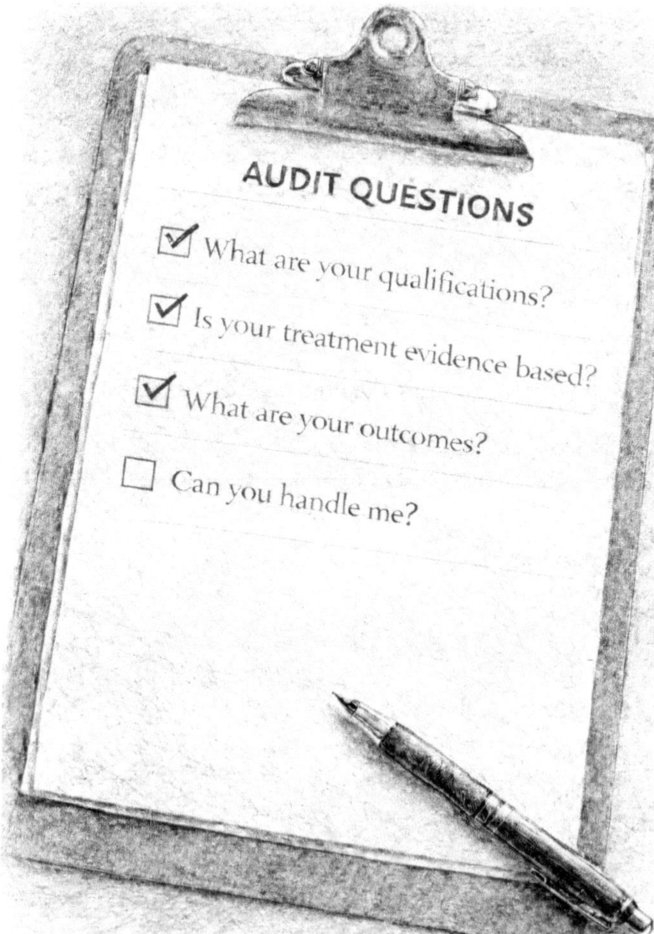
AUDIT QUESTIONS
What are your qualifications?
Is your treatment evidence based?
What are your outcomes?
Can you handle me?

The War Within

"I'm not angry."

His jaw says otherwise.

I see his knee is hammering the underside of his palm.

His shoulders are high and tight—like he's bracing for impact.

"I just get—irritated."

He says it through his teeth.

"Where is it?" I ask.

"Where is what?"

"The irritation."

His eyes flash—quick, defensive.

"It's nothing."

His breathing is already higher in his chest.

I can feel it now—the pressure in the room—

the sense that something is pacing behind his ribs, looking for an exit.

"I work all day," he says, voice tightening.

"I come home and—before I even sit down—someone needs something. It's just constant."

"And what happens inside?"

"I boil.

"Then I handle it."

He says it with a snarl. His fingers curl into fists.

"I don't drop the ball.

I see it. The pattern—competence as containment.

Something in me recognizes the tone—

the performance of steadiness, the refusal to need.

My parts start to stir.

I feel the subtle pull to meet him there—

to be the composed one, the one who guides this cleanly.

Instead, I slow down.

"And if you didn't handle it?" I ask.

His jaw flexes.

"I don't have that option."

The room shifts.

That sentence has weight.

"What would happen?" I press.

His eyes now lock onto mine.

"For who?" he says.

Not a question—a warning.

Silence stretches.

His chest is moving fast now. Shoulders tight. Neck rigid.

"Where is it in your body?" I ask.

He presses a fist into his sternum.

"Here."

"How does it feel?"

"Hot."

"Don't push it down," I say quietly.

"I'm not."

I see his throat struggling to let it come up.

His knee stops bouncing.

Everything goes still.

The air feels charged—

like the second before a storm cracks open.

My heart kicks once, hard against my ribs.

Adrenaline flickers.

I register the size of him—

the intensity in his eyes, the force gathering behind his teeth.

My pattern whispers: Contain this. Manage this. Do not let this escalate.

I do not rush.

"Let it be here," I say. "You don't have to aim it at anyone."

His face shifts.

For a second, I think he's going to shut it down.

Instead—a sound explodes out from inside of him.

Not loud. Not a scream.

Raw. Low. Animalistic—dragged up from somewhere ancient.

It tears through the room.

My body reacts before my mind does—a spike of heat up my spine.

My muscles tighten, breath catches.

There is a flash of thought—This could get out of control.

I stay seated.

I do not lean back.

I do not brace.

I let my shoulders soften deliberately.

I let him see that I am not flinching.

Abruptly, the raw animal sound cuts off.

"Oh my God," he says, eyes widening.

He looks at me like he's just crossed a line.

"I'm sorry. I didn't—"

His hands are shaking now.

"I didn't mean to—"

"Stop," I gesture gently with open hands, remaining steady with my breath.

We both listen.

All is quiet.

Nothing is broken.

Nothing overturned.

The walls are still upright.

I am still here.

"What just happened?" I ask.

"I lost it."

"Did you?"

His breathing is ragged. His chest heaving.

He scans the room again—expecting damage.

There is none.

"You felt something," I say. "And it moved."

His jaw trembles.

"I sounded like..." He struggles to finish.

"Like what?"

"Like I could hurt someone."

The fear is real now. No shame. Fear.

"Did you want to?" I ask.

He freezes.

"No."

Immediate.

"No."

His shoulders drop a fraction.

"What did you feel?" I ask.

He swallows hard.

"Power."

The word scares him.

"And?"

His breath stutters.

"Relief."

There it is.

His eyes fill, not with tears exactly—with shock.

"I thought that if I let it out, I'd destroy everything."

I feel the urge to reassure, to soften, to explain the nervous system response in clean language.

I don't.

I let the silence hold.

"You're still here," I say.

He nods once.

"I'm still here," I reassure him.

He looks at me carefully now—measuring whether I'm afraid.

I make sure I am not performing calm, just being it.

I let him see that I felt it too, that my body registered the intensity, and that I chose to stay.

"You didn't destroy anything," I say.

His fists unclench slowly.

The heat in the room shifts. It's not gone. It's integrated.

"For a second," he says quietly, "I wasn't fighting it."

His back lowers into the couch, as if he's been holding himself upright for years.

"I'm so tired."

Not of his family—

of bracing.

of suppressing.

of fearing his own force.

The war isn't over.

But something crucial just happened.

He met his anger.

And I met my own reflex to control the moment.

Neither of us detonated.

We just stayed.

And the room held.

The Twos

Helplessly Helpful

We sit down at exactly the same time.

It's impressive, actually,

like we rehearsed it.

"So what's the latest in your world?" I begin.

Before I can finish the sentence, she's already halfway into her bag.

"I brought you something."

I blink.

Oh no.

A muffin appears.

Not metaphorically—

an actual blueberry muffin, from the bakery around the corner.

"I noticed you had their bag on your desk last week," she says quickly.

"I hope that's okay."

A full two seconds pass as my therapist brain and my human brain argue.

Therapist brain: Boundaries.

Human brain: Blueberry.

Heat rises in my chest.

It's thoughtful, generous—also intimate, for a room in which I charge by the hour.

I don't reach for it.

I don't push it away.

It sits there, like a tasty relational grenade.

"Thank you," I say—too quickly.

My mind starts calculating.

Do I accept this?

Do I cite my gift policy?

Do I pretend that I don't eat muffins?

Maybe I'll split it.

Half a muffin would feel safer.

She settles back into the couch, as if she's just done something perfectly reasonable.

"How are you?" she asks.

Ugh. I'm exhausted by this muffin,

and we're only 90 seconds in.

My professional part stands up inside of me and smooths its blazer.

Answer well.

Answer appropriately.

Do not unravel over baked goods.

"I'm good," I say.

Good—the most efficient deflection in the English language.

She studies my face.

This isn't small talk. She's orienting to me.

And here's the inconvenient truth:

It feels good.

There is a part of me that enjoys being noticed. Adjusted around. Considered.

That part of me would accept the muffin and call it kind, thoughtful.

There's another part that feels the shift.

The room is no longer symmetrical.

"I'm okay," I add. "Thank you for asking."

Translation: Please stop caring for me. I am supposed to be the regulated one.

"Oh," she blinks.

"My brain just blanked," she says. "What should we talk about?"

I laugh softly.

"That's usually my line."

She exhales, relieved.

"I keep wanting to tell you stories about other people. Give you updates. I don't really know how to talk about me."

Yes. I can breathe again.

We're back in familiar territory.

"You brought me something," I say gently.

"You checked on me...

And when it's time to talk about you, you pivot to someone else."

She considers that.

"I just don't really know how to fill the space with... me."

I notice something else in myself:

the part that likes being appreciated...

the part that doesn't mind being a little special in someone's orbit.

That part is not bothered by the muffin. That part is appreciative.

"Can I say something?" I ask.

She nods, immediately.

"When you start taking care of me," I say,

"I feel myself trying to reorganize the room."

She squints.

"Reorganize?"

"Put everything back where it belongs.

You're not doing anything wrong," I add automatically.

My pattern is showing.

It prefers balance. No pastry-induced power shifts.

I pause.

"That's not the point," I say.

She waits.

"I'm curious what it's like for you when you're not attending to someone else."

She frowns slightly.

"It feels... weird."

"Weird how?"

"Selfish."

The word is sharp. Clean. No smile attached.

"Like I'm just sitting here—taking."

Her hands gesture toward herself.

"Like I'm consuming space."

There's the math—

If I'm not helping, I'm costing.

"I don't want to be someone who just takes."

I lean back.

"Okay. Experiment. For the rest of this session, you don't have to take care of me."

She freezes.

"Oh."

"I promise I'll survive."

She laughs, but it's tight.

"That feels wrong."

"I bet."

The room gets quieter.

She glances at the muffin, then her hands.

"What do I do?" she asks. "I feel like a waste of space."

There's a reflex in me that wants to reassure. Affirm.

Correct the distortion.

My pattern loves efficient soothing.

I wait.

"What happens if you're not helpful?" I ask.

She looks down.

"Then I'm not needed."

"And if you're not needed?"

She exhales slowly.

"Then why would anyone keep me?"

There it is.

No metaphor required.

Just the unmasked fear.

As if on cue, my pen slips from my fingers and hits the floor.

She moves instantly.

Halfway down, she freezes.

Eyes wide.

"Oh my God."

Her body was already there.

Ready.

On call.

"That was automatic," she says.

"Yes."

She sits back slowly.

"I didn't even think."

"I know."

She flexes her fingers.

"I don't know what to do with my hands."

"Let them retire."

She laughs, nervously.

"I keep waiting for you to need something," she says.

"I know."

"And I don't like not knowing what to do."

Helping gives her coordinates.

Without it, she floats.

"If I'm not needed... I don't know what my purpose is."

We let that land.

Not dramatic.

Just true.

By the end of the session, she's relaxed deeper into the couch than when she started—

less perched, less scanning.

Then she stands.

Her eyes drift to the muffin.

"You can have it," she says lightly. "Or not."

Playful.

But testing.

"Thank you for bringing it," I say.

A pause.

"And don't do it again," I say, smiling.

But I mean it.

She nods sheepishly.

She leaves.

The muffin stays.

We stare at each other.

It knows what it did.

Great Sexpectations

He leans forward, elbows on his knees.

Engaged. Prepared. Coachable.

She leans back, like someone who's already tired of explaining something she's explained before.

"I don't think I'm asking for something outrageous," he says.

Already negotiating the value of reasonableness.

Behind my neutral nod, I clock it: when someone opens with, "I'm not asking for much," they are almost always asking for something that feels enormous to the other person.

"It's not just about sex," he continues.

This is how you know it's about sex.

"It's about feeling wanted."

She rubs her temple.

"I do want you," she says.

She sounds sincere.

She also sounds depleted.

"I know you love me," he says quickly. "That's not the issue."

But it is.

It always is.

"What does wanted look like to you?" I ask.

He doesn't hesitate.

"Enthusiasm. Energy. Initiative."

I see her glare.

She turns to him.

"You want a freak show."

Silence.

He blinks.

"What?" he asks.

Her voice isn't cruel.

It's exhausted.

"You don't just want enthusiasm, energy, initiative. You want headstands, a trapeze, fireworks— and a standing ovation!"

I can see the spectacle.

She takes an exasperated breath and continues.

"I'm just over here trying to remember if I switched the laundry." She throws her hands up.

Ugh, I feel her.

He's flushing.

"That's not what I want," he says.

"It kind of is," she says.

My parts and I watch with stillness.

"I just want to feel desired," he says.

"I know," she replies. "But the bar keeps moving."

Her exasperation shows.

"If I'm affectionate, it's not enough. If I initiate once, it becomes the new baseline. If I'm tired, I can feel you tighten."

"I don't tighten," he defends.

"You do."

A moment passes.

"You get quiet," she continues, "and then I start calculating."

"Calculating what?" I ask.

"How much enthusiasm is required to keep him from pouting."

He recoils.

"I don't pout."

She laughs once—sharp.

"You absolutely pout."

Silence.

"I don't mean to," he says.

"I know," she replies. "But it feels like I'm dealing with a kid who didn't get cotton candy at the fair."

He winces.

"I'm not a child."

"I don't want to feel like your mom," she says, voice rising. "I don't want to manage your mood because I didn't say yes or perform enthusiastically enough."

He turns to me.

"I'm literally trying to help lighten the load all the time," he says. "I cook. I clean. I handle bedtime. I take things off her plate."

He looks at her.

"I show up."

There's pride there—

and an invoice.

"And when you do all that," I ask steadily, "what are you hoping will happen?"

"That she'll want me."

"And maybe that she will reward you?" I push.

"Yes," he says embarrassed.

"And if she's tired?"

"It feels like rejection."

"Even if it's because she's exhausted?"

"Yes."

The honesty is uncomfortable—

But seems to earn him some credit.

She leans forward.

"Do you know what it feels like on my side?"

He braces.

"It feels like I'm being measured, gauged."

He flinches.

"I can feel the expectation."

"When you do the dishes and then hover—"

"I don't hover."

"You hover."

He opens his mouth—

then closes it.

"When you offer a shoulder rub that lasts just a little too long," she continues, "it doesn't feel generous. It feels like a down payment."

He winces.

"That's shitty."

"No," she says quietly. "What's shitty is feeling like I owe you something because you folded laundry."

Silence.

"It feels like you perform for me, and you expect me to perform for you.'

"I don't want a performance," he says, somber now.

"You want to feel special," she says.

That lands.

I let it rest there for a moment.

"What are you afraid would happen," I ask him quietly, "if you stopped trying so hard?"

His jaw tightens.

"That it would flatten."

"What would flatten?"

"Us. Our relationship. Our magic."

Ah.

"And if it flattened?" I asked.

"We'd drift."

"And if you drifted?"

His voice drops.

"I'd start to feel useless. Like I'm nothing."

There it is.

"And if you feel useless, like you're nothing?"

A pause.

"Why would she choose me?"

Now we're in it.

It's not libido.

It's relevance.

She softens—but doesn't rescue.

"So, when I'm tired," she says slowly, "it's not just about sex."

He nods.

"It's about whether you still matter?"

"Yes," he says.

"I want you to know something. When you escalate," she continues, "I feel like I'm being recruited into stabilizing you."

He frowns.

"What does that mean?" he asks.

"It means I monitor you. I adjust. I give you enough enthusiasm so you don't shut down."

She swallows.

"I've done that my whole life. Keep things smooth. Keep people steady."

She looks at him.

"I don't want to manage you too, especially in bed."

He looks gutted.

"I don't want to be managed."

I lean forward slightly.

"Can we talk about roles for a minute?"

They both nod.

"When you feel like you're managing him," I ask her, "what role are you in?"

She doesn't hesitate.

"His mother."

He cringes.

"I'm not asking you to be my mom."

"I know," she says. "But that's how it feels."

"What changes in your body when you shift into that role?" I ask.

"I get tight. Like I'm assessing."

"Assessing what?"

"His mood."

Silence.

"And what happens to you as a partner when you're assessing?" I ask.

"I disappear."

"And what happens to desire when you feel like someone's mother?"

She laughs—hollow.

"It dies."

He swallows.

"I don't want that," he says.

"Then stop using sex to measure whether you're appreciated," she says quietly.

She's not upset now.

She's just done.

He tries again.

"I can initiate less," he says quickly. "I can back off."

She closes her eyes.

"That's still you trying to fix it."

He stops.

Helpful has failed him.

I'm twitching inside—solution, reframe, clarity. I want to diagram the loop, then land the insight cleanly.

I resist.

I trust they can see this themselves.

"Move closer," I say.

They hesitate before shifting.

Awkwardness fills the room.

He looks at her.

She looks at him.

He inches closer.

She does too.

“Can I?” he gestures toward her.

She nods.

He takes her hand.

“Let her know what you want,” I say to him.

“I want you to want me without me having to earn it.”

“And you?” I ask her.

“I want to be able to say I’m tired without it meaning I don’t want you.”

He exhales.

“I don’t want to punish you,” he says.

“I know.”

They sit.

Close.

No spectacle.

No cotton candy.

After a minute, he says quietly, “This feels calmer.”

She nods, “Because it’s not trying to prove or earn anything.”

"The pressure's off," I add.

They sit in silence for a while—just holding each other.

For the first time, he lets desire exist without turning it into an expectation.

When they stand to leave, he reaches for her hand again—

not strategically,

not as a cue.

Just because.

And this time,

she doesn't feel like she owes him a show.

The Threes

I'll Be Right There

She's talking about her daughter asking her to play.

"'Mom. Come play with me,'" she says.

Standing at the sink full of dishes, her hands are wet.

Soap slick along her wrists. A mental list scrolls behind her eyes.

Her daughter asks again.

And again.

"One. More. Thing."

The invitations weigh on her.

"I tell her, 'In a minute.' but I don't mean it."

She lowers her head.

"I feel like a bad mom," she says.

Shame fills the room as she continues her story.

"She comes back," she says. "And just stands there—

'Now!' she demands."

I see her chest tightening.

I feel it in mine too—a narrowing.

"I just want to finish the dishes," she says, jaw set.

I notice the spark in me—the urge to make this hour count.

To give her something useful, some relief.

I don't act on it.

"Where are you feeling this in your body?" I ask.

"Chest," she says immediately. "Then my jaw. Then my eyes."

They begin to fill.

Her foot taps against the floor. Fast. Unnoticed.

"What is your body saying?"

"I don't have time. I can't. Not right now."

She stares somewhere past me.

I see her face change.

She says quietly, "she is only little for such a short time."

The guilt hits.

She starts to sob, face in her hands.

"What kind of mother thinks like this?" she asks. "Why does this feel so hard?"

She looks up, her body leans forward.

She's building a case.

She hasn't showered.
She hasn't eaten properly.
There's work to finish.
She's trying to write—to create something that belongs to her.

"And I feel selfish for wanting anything for myself," she says.

Selfish for showering without someone knocking.
Selfish for sitting still.
Selfish for wanting five minutes that don't belong to anyone else.

"I feel like I'm always choosing between them and me."

"And what I choose," she says, "is whatever keeps me from falling behind."

Behind.

Her knee bounces. Fingers smooth the cushion. She repositions.

"I don't know how people just sit," she says. "I get uncomfortable."

Even when she has time, she fills it with something.

A shower becomes quick.
Rest becomes scrolling.
A break becomes catch-up time.

People call her strong, capable, impressive.

Her body never fully lands.

"And then my daughter asks me to play."

"How long does play last?" I ask.

She lets out a short laugh.

"Forever."

"And when you imagine stopping the dishes?"

She goes quiet.

"It feels irresponsible."

Immediate.

"What would it mean to let the dishes wait?" I ask gently.

Her head lifts, sharply.

"Wait for what?"

There's heat now.

"No one is coming to do them."

Her foot starts tapping again.

"It's me," she says. "It's all on me."

The words accelerate.

"If I don't do them, they sit there. If I don't fold the laundry, it piles up. If I don't remember the permission slip, the snack, the birthday gift, the dentist appointment, it doesn't happen."

Her jaw tightens.

"There's no backup plan. There's no invisible team. It's just me."

The gravity meets my body. She isn't defending dishes.

She's defending the belief that she is the load-bearing beam.

I feel the reflex to reassure her. To soften the weight. To prove she's not alone.

I stay.

"I don't get to just... stop," she continues. "That's a luxury. That's for people who have someone else to help hold things."

"You're asking me to let the dishes wait, like someone else is going to swoop in and do them."

A short laugh—humorless.

"No one is coming."

I feel the brunt of her words, the weight of her realization—

I also feel like I just stepped into a hornet's nest.

I feel the sting... and the urge to perform steadiness.

A part of me wants to rescue, to carry something for her.

I don't.

"And if you put the sponge down anyway?" I ask, treading lightly.

Her breath catches.

"Then I'm gambling."

"Gambling what?"

"That nothing falls apart."

"And if something does?"

"It'll be my fault."

There, the pattern.

Responsibility as identity.
Control as survival.

"When did it become all on you?" I ask.

"It's always been me," she says.

Not dramatic. Just true.

"If I slow down," she continues, "everything I've been holding up might fall."

"And what are you holding up?"

She inhales, shakily.

"The house.
The schedules.
The moods.
The peace.
The feeling that we're okay."

Her voice thins.

"And if I stop pushing, I might feel how angry I am."

Angry.

Not at her daughter.
Not at the dishes.

At the years.

"If I feel it," she says, "I might not get back up."

The room grows very still.

"I don't trust that I'll come back from that."

Her hands are quiet now.

No tapping.
No adjusting.

"I've been pushing for so long," she says.

"If I stop, I might realize I'm sad. Or disappointed. Or resentful."

She looks at me.

"And then, who holds everything?"

"You think it's you," I say.

She nods.

"It's always been me."

I feel the echo in myself—the part that knows how to carry momentum, the part that wants to make this session worth her effort.

I let that part soften.

"I wonder," I say gently, "if you have been attending to your own needs."

She looks up, confused.

"I have?"

"Yes," I say. "Just indirectly."

Her brow furrows.

"You rest by making sure everyone else is okay. You feel steady when they're regulated. You feel purposeful when you're needed."

She's very still.

"You get closeness by being useful."

A tear slides down.

"That's not wrong," I add. "It's intelligent. It kept you connected."

Another tear.

"But it's not the same as attending to your needs directly."

More begin to flow.

She grabs a tissue.

Her body is folded in on itself.

"What would that even look like?" she sobs.

There's fear in that.

"It might look like sitting on the floor and playing," I say.

"That's for her," she replies quickly through the tears.

"And what if it isn't?"

A pause.

"What if play isn't just you showing up for your daughter?"

Her breath catches.

"What if it's you showing up for the little girl who learned not to need much?"

Her face changes.

Smaller.

"What would she have needed?" I ask.

"To be chosen," she whispers.

"And what if," I say, gently, "when you put the sponge down... you're not abandoning responsibility?"

She listens carefully now.

"You're choosing you?"

"What if you're feeding something that's been starving?"

"For what?" she asks.

"For joy that doesn't have to be earned—for time that doesn't produce anything, from being small and unnecessary."

Her eyes close.

"I don't even know how to want something without making it about someone else," she says.

"That makes sense," I say. "You learned the safest way to get your needs met was to make yourself useful."

A shaky inhale.

"So, if you rest because your daughter wants to play—that's acceptable."

She nods faintly.

"But if you rest because you want to rest..."

Her jaw tightens.

"That feels dangerous."

"And if you sit on the floor and realize you like it?" I ask.

She swallows.

"I might want more."

"And if you want more?"

"I might have to admit I've been neglecting myself."

I see it all—the grief beneath the competence,

the dishes, still in the sink,

her daughter, still in the doorway.

And nothing has collapsed in this room.

Her back presses more fully into the couch.

For the first time, she gives it her full weight.

We don't make a plan.

We don't optimize her schedule.

We don't solve her time management.

We sit.

Long enough for her to test the possibility that she is not the only thing holding the sky up.

When the hour ends, she stands slowly.

Grounded.

"I'll be right there," she says softly.

This time it isn't a delay.

It isn't defense.

It sounds like integration—

not just to her daughter—

to the little girl who learned to wait.

And I notice, as she leaves, that I did not have to carry the hour for her.

I did not have to make it count.

I just had to stay.

And that—

for both of us

was enough.

The Mistress of Alcohol

Today, he lowers himself—like something in him has already quit.

It's subtle. My body catches it before my mind does.

His spine curves. His gaze drops.

His hands hang between his knees—like they don't belong to him.

There's a dimness to him—like someone turned the lights down behind his eyes.

"I've been drinking."

I can hear the exhaustion behind his words.

We've been circling the affair for weeks. Not the event itself—that part is clear in his telling.

Years ago.
One woman.
One fracture.

He ended it. Returned home. Became attentive, reliable, impeccable.

But lately, we've been circling a confession.

Whether he will tell her.

Whether he can live without telling her.

"How long?" I ask.

"Since then."

Since the affair ended.

"And lately?" I ask.

He hesitates.

My pulse shifts slightly.

"What?"

"Has your drinking changed at all?"

He stares at the floor for a long time.

Then, quietly: "It's... more."

Something sharp moves through me.

"More how?"

"Earlier." He swallows. "Heavier."

The word heavier hangs there.

"When did that start?"

Silence.

He presses his palms together between his knees. His knuckles go pale.

"When we started talking about telling her."

The mistress has taken a new form...and tightened her grip.

I feel it in my body.

As the threat of exposure increases, so does the anesthesia.

As truth gets closer, so does the drink.

Not random.

Strategic.

"She's helping you not tell," I say quietly.

His head snaps up.

"Who?"

"Alcohol."

"I didn't say that."

"No," I reply gently. "You didn't."

But we both feel it.

He looks away again.

"She just makes it manageable," he says

Manageable.

The word lands with weight.

Manageable to live with the secret.

Manageable to postpone.

Manageable to keep the image intact one more night.

"And if you didn't drink?" I ask.

His jaw tightens.

"It would be loud."

"What would?"

"The part that says I can't keep this."

His breathing shifts—faster now.

For a moment I feel something cold move through me.

Not his fear of relapse.

Fear of leverage.

Because the mistress isn't only soothing him.

She's holding something over him.

If you tell, you lose the good husband image. If you don't tell, you lose yourself. And if you try to sit in the tension of that without me, she seems to say, I will make it unbearable.

I feel my pulse quicken.

This is no longer passive sedation.

This is containment.

"You've been drinking more as we get closer to the truth," I say slowly.

He flinches.

"I don't want to blow up my life."

There it is.

Survival.

"And the drinking helps you not do that."

"It helps me function."

"Or it helps you not choose."

Silence.

His shoulders drop another inch.

He looks suddenly smaller.

"If I tell her," he says, "I lose who she thinks I am."

"And if you don't?"

He swallows.

"I lose... something."

He can't say it.

But I can feel it—

Himself.

The mistress protects him from shame.

But also keeps him dependent.

She softens the fear of confession.

But increases the cost of staying silent.

"If you drink tonight," I say, carefully, "what happens tomorrow?"

He stares at me.

"I wait another day."

"And if you don't drink?"

He blinks through some tears.

"I might have to decide."

Ah.

The bottle keeps him suspended.

The longer he drinks, the longer he doesn't have to choose.

But the longer he doesn't choose, the further he drifts from himself.

I can feel how precarious this moment is.

His ego built a solution to survive the affair.

Now, that solution is preventing his evolution.

I regulate my breath.

"You're not drinking because you don't care," I say softly.

"You're drinking because you're afraid of what the truth will cost."

His eyes fill.

"And because I don't know who I will be if she sees all of me."

The room goes very still.

THE FOURS

Cave Dying

"I went cave dying this weekend," she says.

She pauses.

"Cave diving," she corrects herself.

I tilt my head.

"What's cave dying?"

She groans immediately, dragging both hands over her face.

"Oh my God."

I smile.

"No, no," I say. "We're absolutely staying with the first version."

"I hate therapists."

"You say that like you didn't walk directly into this."

She laughs despite herself, then drops back into the couch.

Something shifts in her expression—like some part of her is standing just behind the sentence now, realizing it spoke too soon.

"I guess that says enough about my mental state," she mutters.

"Does it?"

She looks toward the window for a moment, chewing the inside of her cheek.

"Maybe."

The room quiets around us.

She's been coming to therapy for almost a year now. Long enough for me to recognize the exhaustion beneath her humor. The exhaustion of someone who has spent most of her life trying to reduce herself for other people's comfort.

Too sensitive.
Too emotional.
Too intense.
Too much.

People often say these things casually, while slowly teaching someone to distrust their own aliveness.

"What was the cave like?" I ask.

Her whole face changes—like more of her has arrived.

"It was beautiful," she says quietly.

There's grief in the sentence already.

"Tell me."

She leans forward slightly, elbows on her knees now.

"You descend backward," she says. "That's the first awful part." A small smile. "Every instinct in your body is like, Absolutely not. People die doing this."

"Reasonable."

"The rope creaks when you lean back." Her fingers tighten unconsciously against each other as she talks. "And you can hear water before you see anything." She pauses. "The whole cave smells like wet stone."

I realize halfway through her story that I've left the office and joined her in the cave.

"There's this moment," she says softly, "where your feet stop touching anything and you're just suspended there in the dark."

The image lands heavily between us.

"And then eventually your feet hit the wall again," she says. "But now you're underground."

Her eyes drift somewhere beyond the office.

"There were these massive open caverns down there," she says. "Like entire worlds hidden underneath everything."

"I bet you loved it," I say.

She smiles immediately.

"I really did."

"I think..." She pauses. "I think it felt familiar."

Something in my chest tightens a little.

"Familiar how?"

She stares down at her hands.

"Like being inside myself."

"My mom used to tell me I cried like someone had died," she says with a soft laugh. "Even when I was little." She shakes her head slightly. "Everything affected me."

I nod.

"I remember thinking adults were weird," she says. "Like everyone was pretending not to notice things."

"What things?"

"Pain. Beauty. Tension." She shrugs lightly. "The truth, mostly."

The sentence moves through the room cleanly.

"She'd always say, 'it's not that serious.'" Her voice changes slightly as she repeats it. "'You're exhausting yourself.'"

The old sentences still live in her nervous system.

You feel too much.
You react too deeply.
You care too much.

Eventually people stop saying it to you.

And you begin saying it to yourself.

"I remember crying after a movie once," she says suddenly. "I couldn't have been older than eight." A humorless smile crosses her face. "My dad looked at me like I was embarrassing him."

That one lands quietly—because almost everyone knows that look.

"I spent years trying not to feel things," she says softly. "Or at least trying not to show them."

"How'd that go?"

She laughs once through her nose.

"It felt like dying."

The room goes still around the sentence.

True things often do that.
Some people experience emotion as disruption.
And some people experience emotion as evidence they're alive at all.

"When I don't express what I feel," she says, pressing a hand lightly against her chest, "it starts building inside me." Her eyes lower. "Like there's this giant cavern filling with water."

I recognize the sensation.

"It becomes pressure—heaviness," she says. "Grief. Longing. Anger. Beauty. All of it together." She shakes her head lightly. "And everyone always wants me to make it smaller. More manageable. Less inconvenient."

"And what do you want?"

Her eyes fill immediately.

"I want to stop apologizing for having a deep interior life."

The honesty of it hits me squarely in the chest.

I know how many people learned to flatten themselves just to remain tolerable to others.

"I don't even think I was dramatic originally," she says thoughtfully. "I think I was just honest."

A girl who learned her emotional truth disrupted the environment around her.

"You know what the weirdest part was?" she asks.

"What?"

"When we got deep into the cave, they turned off all the lights."

Even her voice lowers when she says it.

"It was completely black." She shakes her head slowly. "I've never experienced darkness like that before."

She pauses.

"And honestly?" A tiny laugh. "My body finally relaxed."

The invisibility felt safe.

"No one could see you," I say quietly.

Her eyes meet mine immediately.

"No one could see me."

No monitoring.
No managing.
No adjusting herself around other people's comfort.
Just breath.
Water.
Rock.
Darkness.

A self existing without negotiation.

"And weirdly," she says, "it didn't feel lonely."

"No?"

She shakes her head.

"It felt clean."

The word lands softly between us.

"I think that's why I said cave dying," she says eventually. "Because feeling things is the only time I actually feel alive." She wipes quickly beneath one eye, annoyed by the tears now gathering there. "And when I can't feel—or when I have to hide it—it's like something in me starts disappearing."

I can feel the room organizing itself around her grief now.

Ancient grief.
The grief of learning your aliveness overwhelms other people.

"How do you survive that?" I ask softly.

"What?"

"Being taught that your depth is a problem."

She leans back against the couch and stares at the ceiling for a long moment.

"I think I keep excavating myself anyway."

The sentence moves through me slowly.

Excavate.

Bring what's buried into the light.

"Not to become someone else," she says carefully. "More like..." She searches for the words. "To uncover something I knew before I started hiding."

The room grows quiet again.

And suddenly I can picture her there:
suspended on a rope,
lowering herself backward into the dark,

heart pounding,
descending into hidden chambers beneath the earth,
feeling the strange relief of finally entering a place deep enough to hold her.

Maybe that's what she experienced in the cave.

Not death.

The relief of finally entering something deep enough to hold her aliveness.

The Man You Script

He arrives six minutes late and enters mid-thought.

"I don't think people actually know who they are," he says, closing the door behind him. "I think they know who they've learned to write."

There is no hello as he drops into the corner of the couch, crossing his legs. His fingers move absently over the seam of a throw pillow like he's searching for the edge of something unfinished.

I feel like I'm late to a lecture I didn't know I was attending.

"The older I get," he continues, "the more everyone feels authored."

I tilt my head.

"Authored?"

"Curated. Revised. Edited for likability." He gestures vaguely between us. "Everyone's walking around as a second or third draft pretending they're the original manuscript."

The room settles around him quickly. Some clients arrive anxiously. He arrives atmospherically. Like the session was already happening before he walked in and I'm expected to acclimate.

"And you're exempt from this?" I ask.

His mouth twitches.

"No. That's the disturbing part."

There's something compelling about him.

I find myself leaning in.

Dangerous.

He notices everything—and he'd love for me to be intrigued.

"I've been trying to write," he says.

His face tightens immediately, like the word itself irritates him.

"I'm supposed to be finishing a manuscript." He exhales sharply. "But every sentence feels contaminated before I even finish it."

"Contaminated by what?"

"Other people."

He rubs at his forehead.

"I can hear every influence. Every writer I've admired. Every professor. Every book I loved at nineteen. I write one paragraph and immediately think: that sounds like

Didion. Or Ellis. Or whoever I absorbed ten years ago." He laughs dryly. "I can't tell if I have a voice or just a collection of echoes."

"And what would happen if your writing sounded familiar?"

"Then it wouldn't be mine."

The answer comes too fast.

Outside, someone walks down the hallway laughing loudly. He waits for the sound to pass before continuing.

"The stupid part," he says, "is that the manuscript is literally about identity."

I smile slightly.

"Of course it is."

"The working title is The Man You Script."

I raise an eyebrow.

"That's subtle."

"I know." He smirks faintly. "Apparently my unconscious has all the restraint of a theater kid."

I laugh before I can stop myself.

His eyes flick toward me, pleased.

Not because I understood him.

Because I joined him.

"The whole thing," he continues, "is about how people perform themselves into existence. How they rehearse personalities long enough that eventually the performance calcifies into identity."

"And you believe that?"

"I think I'm terrified it's true."

That lands differently.

Not intellectually.

Personally.

He looks toward the bookshelf behind me.

"When I was younger, people used to tell me I was different." A small shrug. "Insightful. Old soul. Deep thinker. Whatever version adults use when they want a child to feel exceptional."

"And that mattered."

"Wouldn't it matter to you?"

Touché.
Because yes.
Of course it would.

I think most people want to believe there's something uniquely meaningful about them. Something that separates them from the blur of everyone else.

A specialness.
A wound.
A gift.
A tragedy.
Something.

Without it, we risk becoming frighteningly interchangeable.

"I think," he says slowly, "I built my identity around being original."

He looks down at his hands.

"And now I can't create anything because I'm too busy trying not to sound derivative."

Ah.

Not writer's block.

Identity block.

"If the work isn't completely original," he says quietly, "then what does that say about me?"

The room goes still.

Because underneath all the intellectual language is something painfully simple:

If I'm not uniquely constructed, am I still worthy of being seen?

I notice the familiar pull in myself—the urge to become especially articulate with him. More nuanced. More impressive. As if some part of me wants to prove I belong in the conversation he's creating.

Careful.

Now I'm scripting too.

"You're smiling," he says suddenly.

"I am?"

"Yeah."

"Why do you think?"

"You're entertained."

I laugh again.

"That's probably true."

"You like this conversation."

"I do."

"Because you think this way too."

There's no accusation in it.

Just observation.

Annoyingly, he's right.

I glance toward the window for a second, buying myself time.

"I think everyone scripts themselves," I say eventually. "I think most people inherit roles, narratives, identities… and then spend years mistaking the script for the Self."

"And once you notice?"

"That's the problem."

He smiles at that.

A real one this time.

Or maybe not.

Maybe that's the unsettling thing.

I'm no longer sure where performance ends and personhood begins.

Maybe none of us are.

He leans back into the couch, quieter now.

"I don't know who I am without the story," he says softly.

"What story?"

"That I'm different."

There it is.

Not narcissism.

Orientation.

The organizing narrative around which his identity formed.

The story that transformed loneliness into meaning.

Alienation into uniqueness.

Observation into selfhood.

"And if you aren't?" I ask gently.

His eyes move toward me, then away again.

For the first time all session, he looks young.

Not in age.

In exposure.

"Then maybe," he says quietly, "there's no original version of me underneath any of this."

The words settle heavily between us.

No cleverness this time.

No philosophy to rescue him.

Just a man sitting on a couch, unable to finish writing his manuscript because somewhere along the way, he confused being original with being real.

And me sitting across from him, suddenly aware of all the ways I've done it too.

Manuscript

The Fives

Smitten

She drops into the chair—like she's here to observe, not participate.

"I brought my deck," she says.

Of course she did.

"What? No small talk?" I ask, entertained.

She gives me a look.

"I assumed we'd skip the pleasantries."

"Efficient."

"Always."

There's a flicker in her eye. Amusement.

I gesture toward the table, "What are we doing?"

"Let's shuffle."

She does. Slow. Controlled. Like she's handling data.

"What's the question?" I ask.

She shrugs, "What's happening here?"

"With him?"

"With me," she corrects.

Ah.

She pulls the first card.

The Lovers.

She doesn't react.

"Interesting," I say.

"Is it?" she replies, lightly.

Her face is neutral. Too neutral.

"What do you see?" I ask.

"Choice," she says. "Projection. Idealization. Hormones masquerading as destiny."

Dry.

"And in your body?"

She smirks.

"We're not doing that."

"Why not?"

"Because once you move it to the body, it becomes real."

"So, it's not real right now?"

"It's manageable."

She taps the card.

"He's attractive. Intelligent. Slightly unavailable. The Holy Trinity."

"And?"

"And I'm not stupid."

She pulls another card.

The Page of Cups.

She exhales through her nose.

"Oh, come on."

"What?"

"That's adolescent."

"Is it?"

"Yes. It's naive. It thinks feeling something means something."

She leans back.

"I don't operate like that."

There is a part of me that enjoys this. The sparring. The coolness. The refusal to blush.

Careful here.

"And yet," I say, mildly, "you're here."

"Curiosity," she replies.

"About?"

"Whether I'm being manipulated by my own neurotransmitters."

I laugh despite myself.

"You're romantic," I say.

She glares.

"That's offensive."

"Why?"

"Romantic implies loss of objectivity."

She pulls a third card.

The Devil.

She freezes.

Then laughs.

"That's dramatic."

"What do you see?"

"Attachment. Obsession. Chemistry. Poor judgment."

"Temptation?" I offer.

She raises an eyebrow, "You're enjoying this."

"Maybe."

She studies the card again.

Her tone shifts slightly.

"He texted me at 1:12 a.m."

"And?"

"And I responded."

"And?"

"I did not wait a respectable amount of time."

Ah.

"And how did that feel?"

"Slightly humiliating."

The word is precise.

"Why humiliating?"

"Because I was available."

Hmm.

She pulls a fourth card.

The High Priestess.

She smiles.

"See. Mystery. Reserve. Control."

"That's the one you prefer."

"Yes."

"Over the Page."

"Absolutely."

"And over The Lovers?"

She hesitates.

"...Yes."

But her throat moves.

"What happens if you're the Page instead?" I ask.

"I lose leverage."

"And if you lose leverage?"

"I care more."

"And if you care more?"

She goes quiet.

The snark drops a fraction.

"I'm the one waiting."

"Waiting for what?"

"For him to confirm I wasn't ridiculous."

Ah.

"Ridiculous for what?"

"For feeling it."

There it is.

She doesn't fear rejection.

She fears being foolish.

She taps The Devil.

"This is biochemistry," she says quickly. "Dopamine. Novelty."

"And the heat in your chest?"

She freezes.

"We're not doing that."

"Why?"

"Because if I admit it's physical, I can't out-think it."

There's the crack.

"Do you want to pull one more?" I ask.

She does.

The Tower.

She laughs, sharp.

"Oh good. Ruin."

"What kind of ruin?"

"Loss of composure."

"Loss of control?"

She looks at me.

"Yes."

Silence.

"And if you lose control?" I ask quietly.

She swallows.

"I might actually let him see that I want him."

"And?"

"And then I won't be superior."

I get it now.

The erotic charge she feels isn't sex.

It's surrender.

"And what's wrong with not being superior?" I ask.

She studies me.

"You don't strike me as someone who enjoys not being exceptional."

Touché.

I smile.

"Occupational hazard," I say.

She laughs—real this time.

The air warms.

She looks back at The Lovers.

"If I lean in," she says slowly, "I won't be able to pretend this is intellectual."

"No."

"It will be..."

She doesn't finish.

"Destabilizing?" I offer.

"Yes."

"And exciting?" I add.

Her jaw tightens.

"Don't."

"Don't what?"

"Make it sound romantic."

"I'm not. I'm making it sound honest."

She gathers the cards, nearing defensive.

"This is manageable," she says.

"Is it?"

"Yes."

"But you pulled The Devil and The Tower."

She narrows her eyes.

"You're reading into it."

"Am I?"

Silence stretches.

Finally—

"If I text him first again," she says, "I'll know I'm not in control."

"And?"

"And I'll have to see whether he meets me."

"And if he doesn't?"

She holds my gaze.

"I'll survive."

There's steel there.

And heat.

She stacks the cards neatly.

"I don't know if I'm smitten," she says.

"What would that mean?"

"That I'm willing to look foolish."

She stands.

At the door she pauses.

"If I pull The Lovers again this week," she says, "I'm blaming you."

"Of course," I reply.

VI
PAGE of CUPS.
ERS.

The Orchid

He's mid-sentence when I sit down.

"...which is why I don't think her framing is accurate," he says, not acknowledging the shift from standing to sitting—or me, exactly—as something that might require orientation.

"I've broken what she calls 'disconnection' into categories," he continues. "There are at least three distinct phenomena being conflated."

Of course there are.

"She uses words like distant," he says. "But when I ask her to define that behaviorally, she can't. It's vague. Emotional language without operational clarity."

He takes a breath.

Not a pause.

A refuel.

"So, from my perspective, it becomes difficult to respond to a problem that isn't clearly articulated."

He settles onto the couch, ankle crossed over knee, spine upright.

Contained. Self-regulated—as if nothing inside him spills without permission.

That's when I notice the orchid.

White petals with purple throats, veined and deliberate. Not soft in the way roses are soft. Structured. Architectural, with each bloom balanced on a narrow stem that looks fragile, but isn't.

It's placed precisely in the center of the coffee table.

He hasn't mentioned it.

Orchids are not casual flowers.
They don't tolerate improvisation.
With too much water, they rot from the inside out.
If too little humidity, they crisp at the edges.
They bloom only when conditions are exact.

That's not accidental.

"I'm not cold," he adds quickly. "I'm just not performative."

I open my mouth.

He keeps going.

"I don't exaggerate effect for the sake of connection. I don't inflate emotional states to meet someone else's expectations. I say what I mean. I do what I say. That seems healthier to me."

My mouth closes.

"I don't do things I don't want to do," he continues. "That's a boundary. Boundaries are healthy."

He nods once, sealing it.

I feel talked at.

There's no seam. No conversational handhold. My nervous system registers it first—a subtle retreat—like the air has thinned; I instinctively conserve oxygen.

My chest quiets.
My thoughts sharpen.

Buffering.

"She says you're distant," I manage, sliding the sentence into the narrowest gap between his inhale and his next paragraph.

"Yes," he replies immediately. "But she also says she wants honesty. So, I don't pretend."

And we're off again.

"I don't manufacture reassurance," he says. "If something isn't organically present, forcing it seems counterproductive."

Manufacture.
Force.
Organic.

I glance at the orchid again.

It's alive—but only because someone studied its climate. Measured its light. Monitored its soil. It will not survive in ordinary conditions. It demands calibration.

"I imagine that's been protective," I say.

He pauses—

Actually pauses.

He looks at me, mildly surprised—not because I said something profound—but because I didn't argue.

"Exactly," he says. "So, I don't understand why that's a problem."

He resumes. Logical. Coherent.

He clarifies that he's not avoidant—that term is overused. He prefers to describe himself as discerning.

As he talks, my body works harder to stay present.

I feel myself leaning back slightly. Giving him space. Reducing emotional volume.

Ah.

This is what it must be like to live with him.

The orchid sits between us, beautiful but temperamental. It will not bloom if the room is too loud. It will not survive if overwatered with feeling.

"When my wife gets emotional," he says, "I don't see the benefit of joining that state. It escalates things."

He differentiates between unnecessary escalation and issues that require engagement. He believes in containment. Conserving energy. Not wasting internal resources.

"And when she says she wants closeness?" I ask.

"She wants reassurance," he replies instantly. "Which I don't think should be manufactured.

Manufactured again.

I feel a small tightening in my throat.

"What's happening for you right now, as we talk?" I ask.

He blinks.

"Nothing," he says. "We're talking."

"Yes," I say. "And how is it to talk with me?"

He considers carefully.

"Fine," he says. "You're tracking."

Fine.

I let the word rest between us like a temperature reading.

"I want to try something," I say. "Tell me if it doesn't fit."

He nods once. Curious. Controlled.

"As you're explaining yourself," I continue, "I notice my own system pulling back—because there's very little invitation."

His brow furrows.

"Invitation to what?"

"To come closer," I say. "To participate beyond analysis."

Silence—not empty. Processing.

"I'm not trying to keep people out," he says carefully.

"I don't experience it as intentional," I reply.

He exhales—measured.

“Then what is it?”

I gesture toward the table.

“You brought me an orchid,” I say. “You placed it perfectly—and you didn’t mention it.”

He glances at it.

“It’s easy to care for,” he says automatically.

I tilt my head.

“It requires precise conditions,” he corrects.

“Yes.”

Silence deepens.

“Orchids don’t survive in unpredictable climates,” I say gently. “They need controlled light. Measured water. Stable air.”

He looks at the petals.

"They're resilient," he says.

"They're exacting," I reply.

A flicker in his jaw.

"It feels," I continue, "like closeness in your world works the same way. It can exist beautifully—but only when the conditions are right, when it won't overwhelm the system."

His eyes shift back to mine.

"That's not unreasonable," he says.

"No," I agree. "It's intelligent."

Another pause.

"And," I add softly, "most people don't know how to regulate themselves to orchid-level precision.

He swallows.

"I don't like being overwhelmed," he says. "I've been clear about that."

"When did closeness start to feel overwhelming?"

He opens his mouth.

Then closes it.

This pause is longer.

"My mother's moods were… expansive," he says.

"When she was upset, it filled the house."

Filled.

"And you had to regulate the climate."

A small nod.

"I learned to keep my energy contained," he says.

"It was safer."

The orchid between us suddenly feels less decorative.

It's an ecosystem.

Too much emotional humidity, and something inside him wilts. Too much intensity, and irritation blooms.

"And what happens now," I ask, "if you don't regulate?"

"I disappear," he says quietly. "Or I get irritated."

Disappear.

I feel the echo of that in my own body—the way I almost shrank earlier to match his atmosphere.

"I think," I say, carefully, "that people may meet you by lowering their volume."

He stills.

"That's not what I want."

"I don't think it is."

Silence.

The room feels different now—not warmer, exactly—less sterile. Less tightly held.

"I don't know how to be close without losing myself," he says.

There's no lecture in the words now.

Just vulnerability.

"That makes sense," I reply.

Not analyzing. Not strategizing.

Just acknowledging.

We both look at the orchid.

It's stunning. Controlled. Thriving in its pot of bark and measured moisture.

It will bloom—but only under calm skies.

And for the first time since he arrived, mid-argument, he doesn't adjust the climate.

He just sits there, allowing.

The Sixes

Recess in the Courtroom

She's already crying when she walks through the door.

Tears stream gently down her face. She grabs a tissue before she's fully seated.

I lean forward. Grounded. Present.

"What's happening for you right now?"

"I just got off the phone with my daughter's school."

Her voice trembles.

"She's in trouble again."

Again.

"What happened?" I ask, steady.

"She pushed a girl during recess," she says. "Apparently, it's the third time she's had a 'big reaction.'"

Air quotes. Shaking fingers.

Big reaction.

"I feel like this is it," she says. "This is the part where it shows up."

"What shows up?" I ask.

"The damage."

The word lands like evidence submitted to the court.

She wipes her face quickly, annoyed with herself for crying.

"She's only in second grade," she says. "Second grade. And already getting in trouble regularly."

Already.

Regularly.

"I feel like I'm failing."

"She didn't use to have issues," she continues. "This started after the divorce. After the engagement. After I messed up her life."

The timeline is airtight in her mind. Exhibit A. Exhibit B. Exhibit C.

"I did this," she says.

Her hands are clenched so tightly that her knuckles have gone pale.

I feel my parts stir.

Organize the data. Normalize. Offer developmental context. Rescue her from her spiral—something airtight and efficient.

Instead, I slow down.

"What did the school actually say?" I ask.

"That she's having trouble with frustration tolerance," she says. "That she gets overwhelmed and reacts fast."

A sharp breath.

"That's me."

Heavy weight.

"She's inheriting it."

"Or," I say, gently, "she's seven."

She looks at me like I'm minimizing a felony.

"She didn't act like this before," she insists.

"Before what?"

"Before I blew up her life."

There.

We've arrived.

"I left," she says. "I destabilized everything."

Her jaw tightens.

"My mom always said divorce ruins kids."

The ghost takes a seat at the prosecution table.

"What else did your mom say?" I ask.

"That kids need a stable home. That selfish women chase happiness and drag their kids through chaos."

Her voice goes flat.

"And, now my daughter is pushing kids during recess."

The trajectory in her nervous system is brutal:

Selfish → Chaos → Broken child.

"I will not be her," she says suddenly.

Not angry.

She's terrified.

"I will not be my mother."

Her breathing is shallow now. Quick. As if the verdict is imminent.

I can feel the urgency rising in my own chest—the instinct to dismantle the logic, to present counterevidence, to argue her case, cleanly and succinctly.

My parts wants to win this for her.

I don't.

"When you got the call," I ask, "what did you feel first?"

"Panic."

"About what?"

"That this is the beginning of the story."

"What story?"

"That she becomes the problem kid. That teachers label her. That she's the one parents don't want their kids around. That I'm constantly being called in. That I'm the divorced mom who couldn't keep it together."

Her mind is sprinting a decade ahead, building a case file.

"And then what?" I ask.

Her voice drops.

"Then she resents me."

Ah.

Not behavior anxiety.

Attachment terror.

"What does your daughter say about what happened?" I ask.

"She usually says that someone wouldn't let her play. That she felt left out."

"And?"

"That she gets really mad."

Her voice softens.

"She looks ashamed when she tells me."

She pauses.

"I don't want her to feel ashamed," she says quickly. "I don't want her to think she's bad."

"Did you tell her that she was bad?" I ask.

"No!"

Immediate.

"I told her that I understand being mad. That we need to figure out what to do with it."

She stops.

She looks at me.

"That's different from what my mom would have done."

Yes.

But she can't feel that difference yet.

"She's pushed three times," she says again, like she's restating the charge.

"Yes."

"You don't sound alarmed."

"I'm not."

She stares at me.

"I am."

"I know."

Silence stretches. The courtroom hums.

"What are you afraid this means about you?" I ask, softly.

She swallows.

"That my mess is turning into her mess."

"That I choose men over my child."

"That I'm selfish."

The inheritance speaks.

"If she struggles," she continues, "it proves that my mom was right."

This isn't about recess.

It's about the courtroom in her head.

Her mother is prosecuting. She's both defendant and jury. Every playground conflict becomes evidence.

"What if your daughter pushing a kid means that she felt left out and didn't know what to do with that feeling?" I ask.

She hesitates.

"That's... possible."

"What if it doesn't mean that she's broken?"

Silence.

"What if it doesn't mean that you ruined her?"

Her eyes fill again—softer this time.

"I don't know how to not take it as proof," she whispers.

"I know."

We sit in that.

"You're trying to prevent her from ever feeling what you felt," I say gently.

She nods.

"Yes."

"And when she does feel something hard?"

"I panic."

"Because?"

"Because I think I caused it."

Ah, yes.

The illusion of control.

"If you can cause all of it," I say carefully, "you can prevent all of it."

She looks up.

"And if I can't prevent it..."

"You're human."

Her breath catches.

"You are not your mother because your daughter has feelings," I continue. "You would be your mother if she couldn't bring those feelings to you."

Silence.

"She told me that she was mad," she whispers.

"Yes."

"She didn't hide it."

"No."

"She came to me."

"Yes."

Her shoulders drop, just slightly.

"She didn't protect you from it," I add.

That one hits deeper.

Because she protected her mother.

Her daughter didn't.

"She's not walking on eggshells," she says quietly.

"No."

A long pause.

"She's allowed to struggle," I say. "And you're allowed to not be the cause of every struggle."

The courtroom quiets.

"What would it look like to respond to this as a mother—not as a defendant on trial?" I ask.

She sits with that.

"Call the teacher back," she says slowly. "Ask for more context. Talk to my daughter about what to do when she feels left out."

No catastrophe.

No sentencing.

Just parenting.

She wipes her face again.

"She's seven," she says.

"Yes."

"And I left a marriage that wasn't good."

"Yes."

Both are true.

Her daughter pushed someone at recess.

She leans back.

For the first time all hour,

she isn't on trial.

I Don't Believe In Therapy

He doesn't sit right away.

He steps just inside the doorway and pauses.

Slow scan.

Bookshelves.
Windows.
The salt lamp.
The trailing plants.
The moon phases above the couch.
The faint smell of something herbal.

His eyes land on a stack of cards on the side table.

He doesn't comment.

But he notes it.

"Where do you want me?" he asks.

Neutral tone. Alert body.

"The couch is pretty cozy."

He walks further in now, boots quiet on the rug. Still scanning.

He pauses.

"Do you want me to take my boots off?"

I'm cross-legged in my chair, barefoot.

"Only if you want to."

He continues to look around.

"You weren't kidding about the cottage vibe," he says finally.

I smile.

"It's aggressively non-fluorescent in here."

He huffs once through his nose.

He sits—though not fully back. One foot is planted. One is angled toward the door.

Officer posture in a room that smells faintly like incense.

"I'll be straight with you," he says. "I don't really believe in therapy."

"Neither do I," I reply, straight-faced.

He pauses.

His eyes narrow slightly.

Testing for sarcasm.

I give him nothing.

"My doctor suggested it," he continues. "Says my anxiety's high. Blood pressure's up. Sleep's trash."

A shrug.

"I think that's dramatic. But I listen to my doctor. So, here I am."

He glances around again.

"You don't exactly look like someone who works with cops," he adds.

"Is there a uniform for that?" I ask.

A faint smile.

"You know what I mean."

"I do."

A beat passes.

"Can I ask something?" I say.

He stiffens a fraction. Not defensive—alert.

"Sure."

"Why me?"

He didn't expect that.

He looks around again—slower this time.

"The vibe," he says.

I raise an eyebrow.

"Expand."

He gestures vaguely at the room. "You don't look clinical."

"Thank you."

"You don't look like you're going to pathologize my job."

"True."

He studies the bookshelf. His eyes linger on a labradorite owl, then on the cards again.

"And," he says carefully, "I heard good things."

I wait.

"And?" I ask.

He exhales.

"And you had something on your website about 'internal authority.'"

Ah.

"That phrase caught my attention," he says. "Most therapists talk about coping skills. You talked about power."

Interesting.

"You investigated me," I say, lightly.

"Of course I did."

"Thoroughly?"

"Thoroughly."

I grin.

"And you still came."

A flicker of humor. "That's what's confusing."

He shifts in his seat, finally leaning back half an inch.

"I don't believe in therapy," he repeats. "But I do believe in pattern recognition."

"Go on."

"I've been running on the same operating system for years," he says. "It works. Mostly. But my body's starting to disagree."

"That'll happen."

He nods.

"And," he adds, glancing at the tarot deck again, "I don't think everything is cured by breathing exercises."

I tilt my head.

"No?"

"No."

Silence hangs there.

"You into this stuff?" I ask gently, nodding toward the cards.

He hesitates.

Then shrugs.

"My grandmother read cards," he says. "Didn't call it that. But she'd lay them out at the kitchen table."

That softens something in his face.

"She said that some things can't be approached head-on." He adds, "You have to circle them."

Well.

That's not nothing.

"So, you chose the witchy cottage therapist," I say, "on purpose."

A corner of his mouth lifts.

"I figured if I was going to try something I don't believe in," he says, "I might as well go all the way."

"And?"

"And I wanted someone who wasn't intimidated by authority."

There it is.

"You testing that theory?" I ask.

"Constantly."

I nod.

"Fair."

He exhales.

"You're not what I expected," he says.

"In what way?"

"You didn't flinch when I came in."

"I noticed the exits too," I reply.

That earns a real laugh.

Short. Genuine.

"So," he says, settling slightly deeper into the couch, "you're not scared of cops. "

I'm not scared of people who are scared," I say.

He goes still.

"Is that what you think this is?" he asks.

"I think staying 'on' all the time is expensive," I reply. "And sometimes the people who are the most prepared are the most tired."

A long pause.

His eyes drop briefly to the rug. The plants. The cards.

"You ever read for clients?" he asks, almost casually.

"Not really. I prefer to help them read for themselves," I say.

A smirk.

"Right. Internal authority."

"Yes."

Another beat.

He leans back—not fully relaxed, but no longer angled toward the door.

"You aren't going to send me to the grippy socks motel, are you?"

My eyebrows raise. "Not unless it's necessary."

He smiles.

"My grandma used to say," he says quietly, "that the bravest people are the ones who walk into rooms where they don't control the variables."

He looks at me directly now.

"I don't like not controlling the variables," he says.

"I gathered."

Silence.

"You picked this room," I say. "That's something."

He nods once.

"Yeah," he says. "It is."

For someone who doesn't believe in therapy —

he chose the therapist with witchy cottage vibes, crystals, and tarot cards.

It feels like a good choice.

The Sevens

Sunset

My client walks in, half a step ahead of her wife.

Drops onto the couch.

"Apparently," she says, "we're doing this."

Her wife sits beside her, steady.

"I asked to join," her wife says gently.

"And I agreed," my client replies. "I'm growth-oriented," she says with air quotes.

"You sighed," her wife says.

"That was reflective breathing."

We all smile.

We all know the story of why she's here.

She was seven years old on a park trail. The light shifted. She couldn't see. She froze. Eventually, she was found. Since then, she's had evening panic attacks.

Today, after several sessions of individual therapy, we're visiting the story in a new way.

"When the light starts to lower," her wife says, "she starts preparing."

"I'm just cleaning up," my client says.

"You're discharging your anxiety," her wife clarifies.

"When the light lowers," I ask gently, "what happens in your body?"

She exhales and rolls her eyes.

"Oh my God, I know. I was seven. It was dark. I survived. We've processed this."

She delivers it quickly.

I nod.

"Yes. We know the story."

She relaxes slightly—assuming we're moving on.

"I'm wondering," I continue, "if it would be okay to slow it down today."

Her eyes flick up.

"With her here?" she asks.

I turn toward her fully.

"That's what I want to check. Is it okay with you if we let your body feel some of this while your wife is sitting beside you? We can go slowly. You're in charge."

Her wife stays quiet. Present.

My client hesitates and starts to crack a joke.

Then she nods once and takes a breath.

"Okay," she says.

"Good," I say softly. "And if at any point it feels like too much, you tell me."

"Oh, I will."

"And," I add, "it might matter that you're not alone in it this time."

"Yea, I have witnesses today."

"Your experience is being held," I clarify.

Her wife's hand shifts slightly on the couch between them. Close enough to reach.

"When the sun starts to set now," I ask gently, "what does your body remember?"

She swallows.

"That light disappears," she says. "And I'm alone when it does."

I glance at her wife.

"Would it be okay if she touched you right now?" I ask.

My client exhales—half-laugh, half-nerves.

"Yeah," she says.

Her wife takes her hand.

"What's happening in your chest?" I ask.

"It's tight."

"Is the tightness from now or from then?"

She closes her eyes briefly.

"Then."

"And what's true now?"

She pauses.

"She's here."

"Yes."

"And?"

"I'm not seven."

"Yes."

We sit.

The room is dimmer now.

She notices.

Her shoulders lift.

"I don't like the drop," she says quietly.

"The drop?" I ask.

"When it shifts. When everything gets... thick."

"Let's stay with the thickness," I say gently. "Just for a few breaths. You're here. She's here. I'm here. The light is lowering. And no one is leaving."

Her breathing is shallow.

Her wife's thumb moves slowly across the back of her hand.

"Are you lost?" I ask softly.

She opens her eyes.

"No."

"Are you alone?"

She looks at her wife.

"No."

The silence stretches.

No jokes.

Just her nervous system not evacuating.

"What does your body want to do?" I ask.

"Leave," she says honestly.

"And what are you choosing?"

"Stay."

Her voice is quieter now.

Not dimmed.

Settled.

The light lowers another shade.

Her breathing deepens slightly.

"This feels different," she says.

"How?"

"I'm not fighting it."

Her wife squeezes her hand.

She whispers, "You don't have to fight it."

The sun continues to set.

And this time, she isn't bracing alone.

She stays long enough for the moment to crest and fall on its own.

"I don't want to be ruled by sunset," she says, finally.

She's not conquering it.

Not loving it.

Just not governed by an old rule anymore.

The room grows darker.

She doesn't check the time.

She doesn't suggest we wrap up.

She sits with us,

and lets the light go.

Protecting His Peace

"We're fine," he says easily. "We just argue differently."

He settles into the couch like he's about to host a segment entitled Healthy Conflict Styles for Couples.

Ankle over knee. Arm stretched wide. Relaxed. Warm eye contact.

He's handsome. Charming.

And he knows it—a perfect talk show host.

"She thinks I leave," he says, smiling at me. "I don't leave. I just don't marinate."

Marinate.

Hmm.

"You grab your keys," she says.

"I go for a drive."

"Mid-conversation."

"I need air."

He turns toward me.

"That's healthy, right? Taking space instead of making it worse?"

He's not wrong.

Air is mature.
Air is regulated.

Air is the opposite of screaming in a kitchen at 11:57 p.m.

"I don't see the benefit of stewing in negativity," he continues. "Life's short. Why consume the same feeling for hours?"

Inside, the studio lights warm.

My parts assemble in tidy rows. A few nod approvingly.

He's making sense.

He's speaking my parts' language.

"I take some deep breaths, listen to soothing music," he says. "Clear my head. Come back ready to reconnect."

My parts applaud.

"I come back calmer. That's helpful."

More applause.

She clears her throat.

Applause falters.

"When you leave," she says, sharper now, "it tells me I'm alone in it."

My parts take a collective breath.

He exhales gently.

"That's not what's happening," he says, turning to me, like we're co-hosting this now.

"I'm preventing escalation. I'm the one keeping it from blowing up."

He gestures toward her. Soft diplomacy.

"She feels things big."

Weather report tone.

Not judgment. Just data.

My internal audience perks up again.

"Maybe that's what we should be working on," he says. "Why everything turns up to ten."

He says it kindly. Reasonably. Like he's glanced at a cue card reminding him to mention attachment styles.

I feel myself sliding back into co-host role.

"That's what therapy's for, right?"

Spotlight.

"Yes, I reply."

He nods.

She goes still.

Applause cuts off mid-clap.

The warmth of alignment instantly cools.

F*ck.

"I mean no."

A few audience members look confused.

"I mean… therapy isn't just addressing intensity," I say. "Sometimes it's about understanding why something feels threatening."

The lights dim. The set shrinks.

"When she feels things big," I continue, "what happens inside you?"

The charm softens.

"It feels like I'm getting pulled into something," he says. "Like the whole night becomes about a mood."

"A mood," she repeats.

"Yes," he says. "An atmosphere."

"And when you stay?" I ask him. "What are you afraid will happen?"

His smile thins.

"That I'll disappear," he says quietly. "Like I won't exist in it."

The studio goes dark.

No applause. No cue cards.

They breathe.

She turns toward him fully.

"I don't want you to feel what I'm feeling," she says. "I want you with me while

I feel it."

He studies her.

"And when he leaves?" I ask her.

"My stomach drops," she says. "Like I've misjudged how close we are."

He looks at me again.

"I'm trying not to escalate."

"I know."

He waits.

I don't rescue him.

"I just think taking space is healthy," he says. "You'd tell clients that."

"I do," I say evenly. "And I also tell them that pleasant isn't the same as connected."

The words hang in the room.

They hang in me, too.

He swallows.

"You're very good at keeping it light," I add gently. "It works. It keeps everything manageable."

I hold his gaze.

"And I think it's how you've learned to protect yourself."

The room stays quiet.

"If you can make it reasonable," I say, "you don't have to risk being pulled under."

He doesn't smile.

He doesn't look at me for agreement.

He looks at her.

The vent hums above us. The clock ticks.

She inhales, resisting the old urge to press.

He shifts, resisting the old urge to charm.

They both feel it.

He stays.

Somewhere inside me, the parts that almost launched a show sit down.

No applause.
No verdict.
No hosting.

Just two people sitting in the parts of themselves they usually talk their way around.

That's not peace.

It's presence.

APPLAUSE

The Eights

She's In My Chair

She's already seated when I walk through the door—in my chair.

Not the client couch.

My chair.

Leg crossed. Back straight. Notebook open.

"Oh," she says casually. "I didn't realize."

She knew.

She doesn't move immediately.

I feel it first.
Heat under my ribs. A flicker of alertness.
My nervous system registers it before my thoughts do.

She's a therapist.

This could be an honest mistake.

Or we could be in a duel over the power chair.

I smile as I walk by and sit on the couch.

A beat passes.

She watches me.

Most people would apologize.
Overcorrect.
Scramble.

She doesn't.

"Are you comfortable there?" she asks.

Her tone is neutral. Curious.
But it lands like a probe—

Are you going to assert yourself?

Or accommodate me?

I cross my legs—comfortably.

"I'm good," I say.

Steady.

Another beat passes.

The air thickens—

Activated.

I feel my pattern flex—the quiet urge to demonstrate competence, to win with subtlety.

I let it settle.

"You're checking me out," I say calmly.

Her eyebrow lifts slightly.

"I don't know what you mean."

I smile softly.

"It feels charged in here," I say. "Do you feel it?"

She shifts in the chair, but maintains eye contact.

She pauses.

"Seeing a therapist is awkward for me," she says finally. "I have a healthy mistrust of authority. Apparently, that includes therapists."

"Healthy mistrust," I repeat lightly.

"Yes. Authority gets sloppy. Or self-important. Or fragile."

"And you've learned to stay stronger than it," I say.

She doesn't deny it.

"I don't like depending on people who position themselves as the experts."

"I'm not interested in being your authority," I say.

Her eyebrow lifts again.

"No?"

"No. I'm interested in helping you trust your own."

That hits differently.

She sits back slightly.

"I don't have an issue with my own authority," she says.

"I don't think you do," I reply. "I think you live there. The question is whether it's internal—or reactive."

She leans forward a fraction.

"Explain."

"There's external authority," I say. "Titles. Roles. Power positions. People who claim control."

She glances briefly around the room.

"And then there's internal authority. The part of you that knows what's true without needing to overpower anyone."

Silence.

"You don't trust external authority," I continue. "And your body walked in here ready to defend against it."

"I'm not defending," she says.

"You positioned yourself in the strongest seat in the room before I arrived," I say gently. "That's not dominance. That's protection."

Her jaw tightens.

"I wasn't protecting."

"Not consciously," I say. "Your body moved before your mind did."

"You let me sit there," she says.

"Yes."

"Why?"

"Because if your authority is real, it doesn't need the chair."

That lands.

"And if it's reactive?" she asks.

"It's exhausting," I say. "Because you're not just leading. You're bracing."

Her breathing shifts.

Bracing.

"That doesn't feel inaccurate," she says quietly.

"I don't want to manage my therapist," she adds. "That's why I'm here. I need capacity."

"Do you manage people a lot?" I ask.

"Yes. I get impatient. With inefficiency. With emotional spirals. I tighten. I take over. I push."

Push.

"And when you push?"

"They either rise. Or crumble."

"And if they crumble?"

"I lose respect."

"And if they rise?"

"We get somewhere."

"And where do you go," I ask quietly, "when you're the one crumbling?"

Her posture shifts.

"I don't."

Her policy.

I don't challenge it.

"Your body's still activated," I say gently. "Even now."

"What do you mean?"

"Your shoulders are up. Your breath's shallow. Your jaw's tight."

She notices.

Unclenches.

Then immediately reassembles.

"That's just how I sit."

"Maybe," I say. "Or maybe it's how you stay ready."

"Ready for what?"

"For someone to disappoint you."

She doesn't argue.

"I don't like depending on people," she says.

"Why?"

"Because it sets me up."

She glances away.

"It's risky."

"It feels risky to depend on me right now?"

"Yes."

"That's honest."

"I don't know you. And I don't want to end up managing this."

"This?"

"This room. You."

"That sounds exhausting."

"It is."

There's the crack.

"You're scanning me," I say.

"Yes."

"For what?"

"Whether you'll flinch."

"And if I flinch?"

"I'll take over."

"And if you take over?"

Pause.

"I'll resent you."

"And if you resent me?"

"I won't stay."

Push.
Test.
Take over.
Lose respect.
Leave.

"I won't collapse," I say evenly. "And I won't compete with you. I won't disappear either."

Silence. Longer now.

Less sparring.

"I don't like not being in control," she says quietly.

"What happens in your body when you're not?"

"My chest gets tight."

"Stay there," I say softly. "Don't change it. Just notice."

She resists.

"This is the part I don't like," she says. "The slowing down."

"Why?"

"It feels like I'm losing my edge."

"And what's your edge doing for you right now?

Her eyes glisten.

"It keeps me from looking stupid."

"What would be stupid?"

"Needing help."

Oh.

Need.

"You're very comfortable in protection," I say softly. "But protection and authority aren't the same thing."

She looks at me.

"Authority doesn't have to scan," I continue. "Protection does."

Her breath shifts.

"Authority is grounded. Protection is bracing."

She inhales sharply.

She mutters something through her teeth.

Her spine straightens automatically.

"There," I say gently. "That move."

"What move?"

"The straighten. The control."

Her breath stutters.

Tears spill before she can stop them.

"F*ck," she says, wiping her face angrily. "I hate this."

"You hate what?"

"Slowing down," she says through tears. "If I slow down, I lose it."

"You're not losing it," I say. "You're setting down armor."

She grips the arms of the chair.

"I don't fall apart."

"You're not falling apart."

Her voice breaks.

"I don't know who I am without the armor."

Ah, yes.

Not power.

Identity.

"You're not losing authority," I say softly. "You're just not having to protect it."

She cries.

Angry.

Relieved.

Real.

And I'm still here.

On the couch.

Not taking the chair back.
Not overpowering her.
Not shrinking.

Just steady.

For the first time since I opened the door,

she isn't measuring me.

She isn't bracing.

She's feeling.

And her authority doesn't disappear when the armor softens.

It gets quieter.

Stronger.

Internal.

Because, finally—she's not alone.

High Voltage

I feel the undercurrent before they reach the door.

Some couples argue with shots.
Some with eye daggers.
These two arrive...conducting.

She enters first—shoulders tight, moving fast. Her mind is already mid-task.
He follows a half step behind.

He doesn't greet me.
He scans the room—quickly, efficiently.

Not with curiosity.

With assessment.

Then he sits.
He claims.

With legs wide, arms heavy, he's relaxed—yet immovable. Like the furniture was designed for him.

He's not loud.

Just charged.

The room adjusts.

She perches on the couch, phone in her hand. Thumb moves before she registers it.

Buzz.
She glances down.

"Jesus Christ!" he snaps, low and sharp. "We're paying for this hour."

It lands hard.

But not about money.

His eyes stay on her, a second too long.
Watching what she does next.
Logging it.

My chest tightens.
I breathe.
It passes.

"Yes," I say. "You are."

I swallow.

"And you both get to decide how you want to use it."

He looks at me, sizing me up.

I hold his gaze.

It's not just me he's checking.
He's checking the room.
Who holds. Who folds. Who he has to manage.

Carefully, she sets the phone down.

"I'm tired," she says. "I feel like I'm constantly behind."

Work. Kids. Bills. Logistics. The invisible grid she keeps humming.

"You're gone even when you're here." He says it with voltage.

It sounds like an attack.
It isn't.
It's testing.

"I'm overwhelmed."

"You always say that."

"I am."

"You sound like such a victim when you say that. Take responsibility for yourself. If you're overwhelmed, do something different."

Her jaw tightens.

"Different? How could I possibly do something different? I'm trying to keep everything up!"

She is meeting his charge.

"Let's pause," I say. "I'm guessing this is familiar."

She nods.
He looks at me, like that's what we're here for.

I adjust my feet on the floor.
Take a breath.

"I hear the intensity and frustration in your voices."
This sounds like a painful point for both of you."

A beat passes.

"You're each trying to get met.
And I imagine... trying to meet each other too."

She nods.

He's still looking at me—steady, assessing.

I gesture to him first...

"What do you want from her?"

"I want her attention."

"And when you don't get it?"

"I feel like I don't matter. Like I'm not important enough."

Another beat.

"And like she thinks she's superior."

Something in him lowers.

She chimes in.

"When you're like this," she says, gesturing toward him, "you're not exactly safe to move toward."

He stills.

Not withdrawing.
Calibrating.

"When I'm like what?"

"Like this. You don't yell. But it's there."

He locks in.

"Don't flip this."

"Don't what?"

"Redirect it."

His voice stays measured, which sharpens it.

"I'm telling you I miss you," he says. "I'm telling you I don't feel you. And you turn it into my anger."

"That's not what I'm doing."

"It is."

The air thickens.

"That's disrespectful," he adds.

The word lands heavier than the moment requires.
Not just naming something—correcting it.

"I'm not disrespecting you."

"Yes, you are." His jaw flexes. "You're invalidating what I'm saying by turning it into tone."

He isn't trying to explode.
He's trying to stay in it.

"When you get like this," she says steadily, "I feel like I have to insulate."

"From what? From me having feelings?"

"From the intensity. It feels like if I step into it wrong, it escalates."

"It escalates when you disconnect."

Silence.

Neither of them looks at me.

"It escalates," I say, "when it feels like you can't trust what you'll get back."

He looks at me.

Not defensive.
Interested.

"You come in strong," I continue,"and then you watch."

Silence.

"To see if she can hold it."

His jaw shifts.
Not disagreement.
Recognition.

"You hate when she redirects," I say.

"Yes."

"Because it feels like you're being removed."

His eyes shift.

"And when he comes in strong," I say to her, "you speed up."

She nods.

He expands.
She accelerates.
He presses.
She manages.

"And when you speed up," I say to him,"you get your answer."

He frowns slightly.

"That she's not there."

A beat passes.

"Which confirms what you were already bracing for."

"I'm not trying to disrespect you," she says.

"I know," he replies.

And he does.

"But don't tell me my anger is the problem when I'm trying to tell you I'm hurting."

There it is.

Hurting.

"I'm trying to see if you can actually be here with me," he says, quieter now. "And when you're not... I'm done."

He says it plainly.
Like a fact.
Like a rule that's been there a long time.

She swallows.

"When I slow down," she says quietly, "I start feeling useless."

Useless.

"I keep everything moving," she says. "If I stop, everything feels exposed."

He exhales.

"I don't need you to run the system," he says. "I need you to look at me."

"And I need to not feel like I'm stepping into something that might blow," she replies.

They sit there.

No metaphors.
No diagrams.
Just two people trying not to lose position while asking for contact.

"There's a difference," I say,"
between being indispensable and being connected."

Neither of them argues.

"And there's a difference," I continue, looking at him,"
between asking for connection...
and testing for it."

He holds my gaze.

"Tests have pass or fail," I say. "
Connection doesn't survive that."

The room shifts.

He isn't pushing forward.
She isn't reaching for her phone.

No sparks. No escalation.
Just breath.

They're still wired differently.

But for a moment, neither of them is trying to overpower the current.

And neither am I.

DANGER
DANGER
KEEP OUT
HIGH
VOLTAGE

The Nines

Hot Potato

"I'm not in crisis," she says pleasantly. "I just thought therapy might be useful."

Useful.

I nod.

"What would useful look like?"

She smiles. Easy. Open.

"I'm not sure."

I feel like we're playing hot potato.

It lands in my lap warm and blinking.

"Okay," I say quickly. "Well, sometimes people come in because they feel disconnected, or stuck, or—"

She nods.

"That makes sense."

Not claiming it.

Not rejecting it.

Just... agreeable.

I keep going.

"Or maybe, there's conflict you're avoiding?"

"Could be."

Could be.

I feel it now—the potato getting hotter.

"Tell me about your week." Pivot.

"It was good."

"Stressful?"

"Not really."

"Any tension at home?"

"Nothing major."

She answers everything. Not withholding. Calm. Thoughtful.

But not reaching either.

I'm the only one reaching.

I feel my efforting.

"Sometimes when things are 'fine,' it can mean there's a pattern of minimizing your own—"

I stop.

She watches me pause.

"What were you going to say?" she asks gently.

There's no accusation in it.

Just curiosity.

"I think I'm trying to figure out what you need," I admit.

She smiles. "Isn't that your job?"

There's the potato again.

Is it my job?

What is mine to do here?

I get curious.

"So what made you reach out to me?" I ask.

"You felt calm," she says. "You seemed steady."

> I'm not calm or steady.
>
> I'm scrambling. What do you want!?!
>
> I can feel my parts—which have worked so hard developing my approach and communicating it beautifully on my website—start to get scrappy.
>
> Let me at her.
>
> I take a moment to breathe, re-center.

"And you want... calm?" I ask.

"I have calm," she says lightly. "I just wondered if I was missing something."

> This is my opportunity.

"What do you think you might be missing?" I lean in.

> She shrugs softly.

"I don't know. Other people seem to feel things more intensely. Want things."

"And you don't?"

"I don't feel much or want much."

I want something. To send her to another therapist—someone who specializes in calm.

The silence stretches.

She's sitting comfortably in it.

I'm not.

I start to fill it.

"So when you say that you don't feel or want much, that could mean you've learned to dampen your desires in order to maintain connection—"

There it is. Full interpretive swing, trying to punt this potato out of my office.

Even as I'm saying it, I feel it.

I am performing.

Trying to justify my existence.

She tilts her head.

"Maybe," she says. "I don't feel dampened."

The potato is scorching now.

I realize something sharp and uncomfortable:

She handed me the hour.

And I grabbed it like it was my responsibility to animate it.

"What if I give this back?" I say suddenly.

"Give what back?"

"The direction."

She looks mildly surprised.

"Oh."

We sit.

The room is very quiet.

I can feel my body wanting to move us forward.

She doesn't.

Long pause.

"I don't usually initiate," she says finally.

Facts.

"In most areas of your life?" I ask.

"Yeah. Someone else usually has a preference first."

"And you're okay with that?"

"Mostly."

Mostly.

I resist the urge to dissect it.

"What would happen," I ask carefully, "if no one else initiated?"

She looks at me.

Really looks.

"I'd probably wait," she says.

"For what?"

"For someone to care more than I do."

Ah.

And suddenly the dynamic is obvious.

She's not resisting.

She's waiting.

Waiting for me to care more about the session than she does.

And I have.

My part smiles at the recognition—See? Good therapist. I care about your time and money. I won't waste your session.

I giggle at myself.

And start to relax.

"What if this hour doesn't have to prove anything?" I ask, speaking to myself... and her.

Her shoulders drop a fraction.

"That would be nice," she says.

Silence again.

This time I let it sit.

I don't pick up the potato.

I don't toss it back to her.

I don't interpret it.

It's just a potato.

I notice how uncomfortable it is for me to not be needed. I take the moment to sit with my own stuff.

After a minute she speaks quietly.

"I think I've spent my life being easy."

I light up inside, but I don't lunge at it.

"And being easy," she continues, "means I don't have to want much."

Mmm, yes. There's the ember.

Small.

Real.

Coming to this session alone was her doing something significant. Acknowledging a need, a desire.

I nod.

"That feels important."

She studies me, like she's checking if I'm going to make this a thing.

I don't.

At the end of the hour, she stands.

"This was useful," she says.

I almost laugh.

I can feel the exhaustion in my body from my efforts to perform therapy.

"I'm glad you feel that way," I reply.

She smiles.

And I realize the hot potato was never about her lacking content.

It was about my need to supply it.

F*ck.

Taking Up Space

He settles into the couch the way he always does—gently, like he's careful not to crease anything.

Not the cushion.
Not the air.
Not me.

"How's the week been?" I ask.

"Busy," he says. "But good. I mean, not good-good. Just... normal."

He shrugs.

"It's not a big deal."

With him, that phrase doesn't mean dismissal.

It means compression.

"My partner thinks I should push for a promotion. Or something."

Like it's a decorative suggestion.

"And you?" I ask.

"I don't know. Things are fine. I don't want to make it weird."

Make it weird.

He's sitting on the very edge of the couch.
Knees close together.
Ankles tucked back.
Hands folded tightly between his knees.

He looks comfortable.

He is not comfortable.

I notice it and reorient us to what's happening in the room.

"Can we try something?" I ask.

He nods easily.

"Sure."

"Lean back."

He glances behind him, like he's checking whether there's room.

"There's more couch behind you," I say gently.

A faint smile. He scoots back an inch.

"That's not leaning," I say softly.

Another inch.

His shoulders rise as his back makes contact with the cushion, like his body doesn't quite trust what it's touching.

"Let your spine rest," I say.

He exhales, but his stomach tightens. I can see it through the subtle shift in his shirt.

"What are you noticing?" I ask.

He shrugs slightly.

"It just feels... different."

"Different how?"

A long pause.

"Like I'm on display."

I let the words sit.

"On display to whom?" I ask.

He looks at me, then away.

"I don't know. You, I guess."

"And what happens if I see you?"

His jaw tightens. His shoulders inch forward again.

"Stay back," I say gently.

He keeps contact with the cushion.

His breathing gets shallow.

"It feels like I'm doing something wrong," he says finally.

Sitting.
Resting.
Occupying.

"What feels wrong?" I ask.

"Taking up the whole back of the couch," he says, almost embarrassed.

"The couch is built to be taken up," I reply.

He laughs softly, but his body doesn't fully relax.

I feel my pattern spike—the inefficiency of the self-minimizing, the years of muted ambition, the obvious leadership sitting right in front of me.

My body wants to accelerate this.

Instead, I slow my voice.

"What happens inside you when you let yourself take up more space?" I ask.

He closes his eyes briefly, tracking.

"It feels... risky."

"Risky how?"

He searches.

"Like someone could decide I shouldn't."

"Shouldn't what?" I ask.

"Be that big."

Big.

We sit in that.

His ego didn't announce itself.
It rarely does.

It came in saying, things are fine.

"You learned somewhere that being big costs something," I say gently.

He nods slowly.

"I think when I was younger, whenever I pushed for something... it just created tension. It was easier to not need as much."

"And now?" I ask.

He opens his eyes.

"Now I don't even know what I need."

The room quiets.

This is the edge.

Not conflict with his boss.
Not frustration with his partner.

Disconnection from desire.

"Stay leaned back," I say softly. "Don't move yet."

He nods.

"What do you notice now?"

"My chest feels tight," he says. "But also... I feel more awake."

Awake.

"Yes," I say. "Activation isn't the same as danger."

He swallows.

"It feels like danger."

"I know."

We let it be there.

His breathing slowly deepens.
His shoulders drop a fraction.
His legs extend slightly—almost unconsciously.

He's occupying the couch now.

Not because he decided to be bold.

Because his nervous system realized it could survive contact.

"If you let yourself want more at work," I say gently, "would it feel like this?"

He nods immediately.

"Yes."

"Exposed?"

"Yes."

"Risky?"

"Yes."

"And also a little more awake?"

He pauses.

"...Yeah."

That's the bridge.

"You're not afraid of the promotion," I say quietly. "You're afraid of being seen wanting it."

He goes still.

"That's true."

The words come slower now.

"I think I've believed for a long time that you can't want more here."

"Here?" I ask.

"Any place where I'm not the one in charge.

Work. Relationships.

If I want more, I change the balance."

"And changing the balance feels—?"

"Dangerous."

He doesn't shrink this time.

He stays leaned back.

Breathing.

My pattern hums in my chest again—not impatient now, just energized by his presence. This is the movement I respect.

"You don't have to dominate to take up space," I say.

He nods.

"But you do have to tolerate being defined."

Defined as someone who wants.
Defined as someone with ambition.
Defined as someone who might disappoint.
He inhales.
Long.
Steady.

"I think I've been confusing peace with invisibility," he says.

We let that land.

The hour is ending.

He stands slowly.

His back had been resting against the couch for nearly fifteen minutes.

That matters.

"Pause," I say gently as he adjusts his clothing.

He looks at me.

"Before you go anywhere, feel your feet."

He stops.

His eyes drop.

"Both of them."

He shifts slightly, redistributing his weight.

"Tell me when you can feel the floor."

A breath.

"...Yeah."

"What do you notice?"

"I feel steadier."

"Let your shoulders drop."

They lower a fraction.

He exhales.

"Notice if there's any part of you trying to rush out of here."

A small, knowing smile.

"Yeah."

"Where?"

"Chest. It wants to tighten."

"Stay with it," I say. "Don't fix it."

His hand lifts toward his sternum, then falls.

"It's not as bad as I thought," he says quietly.

"Most activation isn't," I reply. "It just feels louder when you're used to staying quiet."

He nods.

We stand there for another breath.

"You don't have to walk out differently," I say. "You don't have to prove anything."

He listens closely.

"But when you feel yourself perch," I continue, "see if you can let your back find the support again."

He inhales.

"Even if someone's uncomfortable?"

"Yes."

"Even if I am?"

"Yes."

His jaw tightens—then softens.

"That's going to feel exposed."

"It might," I say. "Exposure isn't the same as danger."

He absorbs that.

"Right now," I add, "you're standing in the middle of the room. Not leaning forward. Not shrinking back. Just... here."

He looks down at his stance, like he's surprised by it.

"I didn't realize how much energy it takes to hold myself in," he says.

"It's a full-time job," I reply gently.

A small laugh.

"And if you let some of that go?"

He rolls his shoulders slowly.

"I feel bigger."

"Does bigger feel aggressive?"

He checks.

"No."

"What does it feel like?"

He takes a moment.

"Honest."

Yes.

"Keep that," I say quietly. "The honesty."

He nods.

He reaches for the door.

His spine is upright.
His breath is slower.
His steps aren't rushed.

"Whatever room you walk into next," I say softly,"see if you can let your back touch the chair."

He smiles.

Circling

One Final Session—Mine

On the day this book officially moved forward, I had my own therapy, where I returned to something from my session the week before...

I had told my therapist that I felt like I was circling something...
orbiting a decision...
passing the same point again and again without landing.

I told myself that I didn't know what it was.

Shannon didn't try to rescue me with insight.

In this session, she offered me a three-card spread, asking:

What am I circling?
What is blocking me from seeing it?
What would one step toward it look like?

I pulled:

The Tower reversed.
The Eight of Wands reversed.
Strength upright.

She pulled three cards beside mine:

The Eight of Cups upright.
The Three of Wands reversed.
The Four of Cups upright.

For clarification on the Tower reversed, I pulled:

The High Priestess reversed.

The room went quiet—the kind of quiet that doesn't rush to fill itself.

And then,

"F*ck," I said.

The reversals weren't indicating Uncertainty.

They were showing my hesitation—Energy gathered, but withheld.

The Tower reversed wasn't disaster.
It was dismantling without spectacle.
Holding the structure together just a little longer—
refining, instead of risking.

The Eight of Wands reversed wasn't lack of clarity—
but propulsion stalled on the edge.

The Three of Wands reversed wasn't lack of vision—
it was standing at the shoreline, refusing to board the ship.

And the High Priestess reversed wasn't that I didn't know.
I knew—
but didn't want to say it out loud.

I had been coming close, pulling back, tightening, refining—telling myself that I needed one more pass...
one more improvement...

one more reason to wait...

Because this is my first book.
Because the title is strong.
Because, what if I miss the chance to make it the best it can be?

But "the best it can be" is a moving target, perpetually out of reach.

You can refine a book forever.
There will always be another layer that promises certainty.

Books aren't finished when they're perfect.
They're finished when they're true.

And this one was already breathing.

That's when the quieter fear surfaced.

Not the fear that it wasn't ready.
The fear that I was.

What if I put this out there, and it changes nothing?
What if I step fully into visibility, and the room stays quiet?

What if no one notices?

Somewhere early on, I learned that impact equals safety.
Being exceptional meant not being invisible.
If I was impressive enough, I would matter.

My circling wasn't from confusion.
It was protection.

I don't get to control how this book is received.
I only get to decide whether I stay with what's true.

And truth—unlike polish—requires release and trust.

So, this is me stepping out of the circle.

Before You Go

Yes, you can say f*ck in here.
But that was never the risk.

The real risk is telling the truth in a place where it costs you something—

not in my office,
not in the safety of a paid hour,
not when you know I won't leave.

Out there—

with the person who might withdraw,
with the boss you've been performing for,
with the family system that taught you to edit yourself.

First, your body has to learn what's real:

Telling the truth may change a relationship—
but it doesn't require you to disappear.

Honesty might reveal who can meet you—
and who can't.

You can say what is true,
and stay with yourself—

even if someone else can't stay with you.

And then, one day, almost unnoticeably—

You don't flinch.
You don't retract.
You don't over-explain.
You don't perform your competence before you speak.

You just tell the truth.
And your body learns that you survived.

That's when you don't enter this room in the same way anymore.

About the Author

Katie Fields is a licensed therapist and the creator of CounSouling®, a developmental spiritual psychology that builds ego literacy and integration, helping people move from rigid survival strategies to internally-led, relationally grounded living.

Her work centers on a simple, yet confronting truth: we survived by becoming who we needed to be. And we heal by increasing our capacity to be who we truly are.

Trauma-informed and relational, her clinical approach integrates nervous system science, attachment theory, Internal Family Systems, and the Enneagram, as a map of adaptive intelligence, rather than fixed personalities. She works at the intersection of ego development, regulation, and meaning-making, helping protective patterns soften, as safety, awareness, and choice expand.

Photo by Amanda Allen

What's Next...

*You Can Say F*ck in Here* is an invitation—an invitation into vulnerability and honesty.

My hope is that these stories have connected with you and that the "Oh f*ck!" moments you witnessed here have stirred something honest within you. They certainly have in me.

Now, my own "Oh f*ck!" moment is staying with what comes next, without rushing to define it.

I want to continue this conversation. As our work evolves (yours and mine), I want to stay connected with you.

If you'd like to stay in touch, explore further resources, or follow where this work is going next, you can find me at:

https://www.counsouling.com/

Know that wherever you are, as you close this book—moving, resting, unsettled, or quiet—that is enough.

The work is already happening.

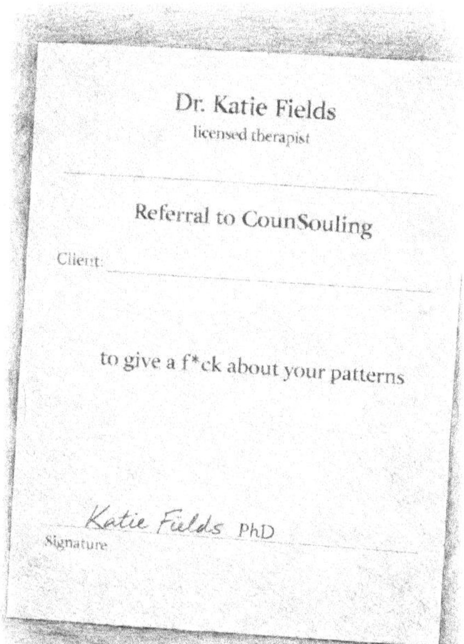

www.ingramcontent.com/pod-product-compliance
Lightning Source LLC
LaVergne TN
LVHW052306200926
848481LV00002B/484
9798996256419